SEEKING
Scripture

2025

This journal belongs to:

_____

If found, please contact:

_____

©2024 Christy Jordan, all rights reserved.

Copyright © 2024 by Christy Jordan
All rights reserved.

No portion of this book may be reproduced in any form without written permission from the publisher or author, except as permitted by U.S. copyright law.

SEEKING SCRIPTURE®

The Seeking Scripture name and logo are registered trademarks.

1st Edition, 2024
Hardback ISBN 979-8-9919225-0-0
Paperback ISBN 979-8-9919225-1-7

Table of contents

Forward 4

Tips for Success 5

How to Use this Journal 6

Daily Pages 8

Additional Notes Pages 373

Learn about Seeking Scripture 399

Reading Checklist for Each Book 400

Foreward

I live in anticipation of the day our Messiah returns. I look forward to being united with my brethren in His eternal kingdom, serving one another out of love, and worshiping Him together. I eagerly await a time when the world will be at peace and we will no longer need to teach others about the Father because everyone will know Him, from least to greatest (Jeremiah 31:34).

Until that time comes, I am so grateful for the wonderful community the Father has given us through Seeking Scripture. In this community, I have tasted a wondrous glimpse of what this future with Messiah will be like. Regrettably, it is a rarity in our time for a diverse group of believers to live in harmony with one another…but when you know God, anything is possible! By His gracious hand, we have formed a loving community of believers from all walks of the Christian faith, seemingly every denomination under the sun. Together, we encourage one another as we deepen our faith by growing in knowledge and understanding of the whole Bible.

Whether you have been with us for years or if this book is our first introduction, it is an honor to study our Father's Word alongside you. Our singular goal is to help you read the whole Bible for yourself. In doing so, we know you will be drawn closer to the Father, developing that first hand relationship with Him that we all long for and need, both in this life and through eternity.

To learn more about Seeking Scripture, check out our charter statements found at the end of this book or visit us at SeekingScripture.com.

Together, may we bring further honor and glory to His name.

Sincerely,

Christy Jordan

SEEKING SCRIPTURE

Tips For Success

1. Choose a Bible translation that works for you.
The BEST translation is one you will read. Check out Biblegateway.com or Biblehub.com to read several translations of a single verse and see which makes more sense to you.

2. Consider large print.
No matter your age, Bible print is tiny! Large print is much easier to read and can make time in the Word far more enjoyable.

3. Keep Reading!
Dedicate yourself to reading daily, but if you miss a few days, don't berate yourself. Self condemnation can easily bring your Bible reading to a standstill. Instead, show yourself grace (It happens to all of us!) and just dive right back in. If you are reading along with the group, begin right where we are; you can pick up what you missed in the next reading cycle. After all, the goal is not to just read the Bible once but to become daily Bible readers.

4. Choose a time that works best for you.
Some prefer to read first thing in the morning, others find they retain more if they read in the evenings. Choose the time that works best for you and do not feel like you are falling short if you find your best reading times differ from others.

5. Make God a priority.
Each day, we make time for the things that are important to us: television shows, Facebook, nightly news, etc. The Creator of the Universe deserves a spot at the top of that list. I want to encourage you to make a date with God each day *and don't stand Him up!*

6. GET EXCITED!
If you've found the Word of God to be dry and impersonal in the past, get ready for all of that to change. We are going to begin at the beginning and experience the Word coming to LIFE like never before and give life to these dry bones!
God's Word is ALIVE, get ready to feel it!

How to use this journal

It is my hope that this journal will become one you want to visit daily, thereby helping you develop and maintain a consistent pattern of daily Bible reading.

Each day contains reading assignments accompanied by a QR code that will take you to my notes for that day's readings. My sincere hope is not that you will always agree with my conclusions, but that through my notes you will learn how to study the Bible for yourself, dig deeper, and test everything to the straight edge of His word.

Use the **notes and reflections section** to make short notes of what stood out to you, list questions for which you hope to find answers, or topics you'd like to dig deeper on.

Also included in each page is a **verse of the day** from each day's readings, with a box to write it out if you would like. If you've never set aside daily time to write out Scripture, you may find it both comforting and satisfying. If you prefer not to, this box can be used to list cross references, to-do lists for the day, or in whatever manner is most useful to you.

Utilize the **weather check boxes** to keep a record of your current environment or get creative and use them to indicate the state of your heart as you read that day.

A **gratitude box** will help you develop a grateful mindset as you continually consider new things to be thankful for.

Each day's **prayer box** can be used to note requests, answered prayers, and ways in which you are placing our hope in the Father for His will and guidance in your life.

And lastly, don't be hesitant about filling in the pages however you wish. Make mistakes and scratch them out or erase them if you like. Write in the margins, ignore the lines if you'd like, and utilize this book as a primary tool while you study the Word.

With just a few minutes each day, this journal will become a treasured keepsake of a year in the life of a maturing believer and a precious time capsule of the relationship between a child and their heavenly Father.

This is what YHWH says:
"Stand at the crossroads and look; ask for the ancient paths, ask where the good way is, and walk in it, and you will find rest for your souls."

Jeremiah 6:16

"I, YHWH, do not change."

Malachi 3:6

Who is YHWH?

SEEKING  SCRIPTURE

Wednesday, January 1, 2025

Genesis 1-3

NOTES AND REFLECTIONS

Study Notes

VERSE OF THE DAY GENESIS 2:7

PRAYER & PRAISE

TODAY I'M GRATEFUL FOR

1.

2.

3.

SEEKING SCRIPTURE

Thursday, January 2, 2025

NOTES AND REFLECTIONS **Genesis 4-7**

Study Notes

VERSE OF THE DAY GENESIS 5:2

PRAYER & PRAISE

TODAY I'M GRATEFUL FOR

1.

2.

3.

SEEKING  SCRIPTURE

Friday, January 3, 2025

Genesis 8-11

NOTES AND REFLECTIONS

Study Notes

VERSE OF THE DAY GENESIS 9:16

TODAY I'M GRATEFUL FOR

1.

2.

3.

PRAYER & PRAISE

SEEKING  SCRIPTURE

Saturday, January 4, 2025

NOTES AND REFLECTIONS   Genesis 12-15

Study Notes

VERSE OF THE DAY GENESIS 15:5

PRAYER & PRAISE

TODAY I'M GRATEFUL FOR

1.

2.

3.

SEEKING  SCRIPTURE

Sunday, January 5, 2025

Genesis 16-18

NOTES AND REFLECTIONS

Study Notes

VERSE OF THE DAY GENESIS 18:14

PRAYER & PRAISE

TODAY I'M GRATEFUL FOR

1.

2.

3.

SEEKING SCRIPTURE

Monday, January 6, 2025

NOTES AND REFLECTIONS							Genesis 19-21

Study Notes

VERSE OF THE DAY GENESIS 21:33

PRAYER & PRAISE

TODAY I'M GRATEFUL FOR

1.

2.

3.

SEEKING SCRIPTURE

Tuesday, January 7, 2025

Genesis 22-24

Study Notes

NOTES AND REFLECTIONS

VERSE OF THE DAY GENESIS 22:14

PRAYER & PRAISE

TODAY I'M GRATEFUL FOR

1.

2.

3.

SEEKING  SCRIPTURE

Wednesday, January 8, 2025

NOTES AND REFLECTIONS　　　　　　　　　　**Genesis 25-26**

Study Notes

VERSE OF THE DAY GENESIS 26:24

PRAYER & PRAISE

TODAY I'M GRATEFUL FOR

1.

2.

3.

SEEKING  SCRIPTURE

Thursday, January 9, 2025

Genesis 27-29

NOTES AND REFLECTIONS

Study Notes

VERSE OF THE DAY GENESIS 28:17

TODAY I'M GRATEFUL FOR

1.

2.

3.

PRAYER & PRAISE

SEEKING SCRIPTURE

Friday, January 10, 2025

NOTES AND REFLECTIONS　　　　　　　　Genesis 30-31

Study Notes

VERSE OF THE DAY GENESIS 31:3

PRAYER & PRAISE

TODAY I'M GRATEFUL FOR

1.

2.

3.

SEEKING SCRIPTURE

Saturday, January 11, 2025

Genesis 32-34

NOTES AND REFLECTIONS

Study Notes

VERSE OF THE DAY GENESIS 32:28

PRAYER & PRAISE

TODAY I'M GRATEFUL FOR

1.

2.

3.

SEEKING SCRIPTURE

Sunday, January 12, 2025

NOTES AND REFLECTIONS Genesis 35-37

Study Notes

VERSE OF THE DAY GENESIS 35:12

PRAYER & PRAISE

TODAY I'M GRATEFUL FOR

1.

2.

3.

SEEKING  SCRIPTURE

Monday, January 13, 2025

Genesis 38-40

NOTES AND REFLECTIONS

Study Notes

VERSE OF THE DAY GENESIS 39:3

PRAYER & PRAISE

TODAY I'M GRATEFUL FOR

1.

2.

3.

SEEKING SCRIPTURE

Tuesday, January 14, 2025

NOTES AND REFLECTIONS   Genesis 41-42

Study Notes

VERSE OF THE DAY GENESIS 41:38

PRAYER & PRAISE

TODAY I'M GRATEFUL FOR

1.

2.

3.

SEEKING  SCRIPTURE

Wednesday, January 15, 2025

Genesis 43-45

NOTES AND REFLECTIONS

Study Notes

VERSE OF THE DAY GENESIS 45:5

PRAYER & PRAISE

TODAY I'M GRATEFUL FOR

1.

2.

3.

SEEKING  SCRIPTURE

Thursday, January 16, 2025

NOTES AND REFLECTIONS   **Genesis 46-47**

Study Notes

VERSE OF THE DAY GENESIS 46:27

PRAYER & PRAISE

TODAY I'M GRATEFUL FOR

1.

2.

3.

SEEKING  SCRIPTURE

Friday, January 17, 2025

Genesis 48-50

NOTES AND REFLECTIONS

Study Notes

VERSE OF THE DAY GENESIS 50:25

PRAYER & PRAISE

TODAY I'M GRATEFUL FOR

1.

2.

3.

SEEKING SCRIPTURE

Saturday, January 18, 2025

NOTES AND REFLECTIONS   Exodus 1-3

Study Notes

VERSE OF THE DAY EXODUS 3:15

PRAYER & PRAISE

TODAY I'M GRATEFUL FOR

1.

2.

3.

SEEKING SCRIPTURE

Sunday, January 19, 2025

Exodus 4-6

NOTES AND REFLECTIONS

Study Notes

VERSE OF THE DAY EXODUS 6:7

PRAYER & PRAISE

TODAY I'M GRATEFUL FOR

1.

2.

3.

SEEKING  SCRIPTURE

Monday, January 20, 2025

NOTES AND REFLECTIONS   Exodus 7-9

Study Notes

VERSE OF THE DAY EXODUS 9:20-21

PRAYER & PRAISE

TODAY I'M GRATEFUL FOR

1.

2.

3.

SEEKING SCRIPTURE

Tuesday, January 21, 2025

Exodus 10-12

NOTES AND REFLECTIONS

Study Notes

VERSE OF THE DAY EXODUS 12:12

PRAYER & PRAISE

TODAY I'M GRATEFUL FOR

1.

2.

3.

SEEKING  SCRIPTURE

Wednesday, January 22, 2025

NOTES AND REFLECTIONS **Exodus 13-15**

Study Notes

VERSE OF THE DAY EXODUS 15:11

PRAYER & PRAISE

TODAY I'M GRATEFUL FOR

1.

2.

3.

SEEKING SCRIPTURE

Thursday, January 23, 2025

Exodus 16-18

NOTES AND REFLECTIONS

Study Notes

VERSE OF THE DAY EXODUS 16:27

PRAYER & PRAISE

TODAY I'M GRATEFUL FOR

1.

2.

3.

SEEKING  SCRIPTURE

Friday, January 24, 2025

NOTES AND REFLECTIONS Exodus 19-21

Study Notes

VERSE OF THE DAY EXODUS 20:20

PRAYER & PRAISE

TODAY I'M GRATEFUL FOR

1.

2.

3.

SEEKING SCRIPTURE

Saturday, January 25, 2025

Exodus 22-24

NOTES AND REFLECTIONS

Study Notes

VERSE OF THE DAY EXODUS 24:12

TODAY I'M GRATEFUL FOR

1.

2.

3.

PRAYER & PRAISE

SEEKING SCRIPTURE

Sunday, January 26, 2025

NOTES AND REFLECTIONS　　　　　　　　　Exodus 25-27

Study Notes

VERSE OF THE DAY EXODUS 25:2

PRAYER & PRAISE

TODAY I'M GRATEFUL FOR

1.

2.

3.

SEEKING SCRIPTURE

Monday, January 27, 2025

Exodus 28-29

NOTES AND REFLECTIONS

Study Notes

VERSE OF THE DAY EXODUS 28:36

PRAYER & PRAISE

TODAY I'M GRATEFUL FOR

1.

2.

3.

SEEKING SCRIPTURE

Tuesday, January 28, 2025

NOTES AND REFLECTIONS　　　　　　　　　*Exodus 30-32*

Study Notes

VERSE OF THE DAY EXODUS 33:19

PRAYER & PRAISE

TODAY I'M GRATEFUL FOR

1.

2.

3.

SEEKING  SCRIPTURE

Wednesday, January 29, 2025

Exodus 33-35

NOTES AND REFLECTIONS

Study Notes

VERSE OF THE DAY EXODUS 34:6

PRAYER & PRAISE

TODAY I'M GRATEFUL FOR

1.

2.

3.

SEEKING  SCRIPTURE

Thursday, January 30, 2025

NOTES AND REFLECTIONS   Exodus 36-38

Study Notes

VERSE OF THE DAY EXODUS 36:2

PRAYER & PRAISE

TODAY I'M GRATEFUL FOR

1.

2.

3.

SEEKING SCRIPTURE

Friday, January 31, 2025

Exodus 39-40

NOTES AND REFLECTIONS

Study Notes

VERSE OF THE DAY EXODUS 40:16-17

PRAYER & PRAISE

TODAY I'M GRATEFUL FOR

1.

2.

3.

SEEKING  SCRIPTURE

Saturday, February 1, 2025

NOTES AND REFLECTIONS **Leviticus 1-4**

Study Notes

VERSE OF THE DAY LEVITICUS 2:3

PRAYER & PRAISE

TODAY I'M GRATEFUL FOR

1.

2.

3.

SEEKING SCRIPTURE

Sunday, February 2, 2025

Leviticus 5-7

NOTES AND REFLECTIONS

Study Notes

VERSE OF THE DAY LEVITICUS 7:16

PRAYER & PRAISE

TODAY I'M GRATEFUL FOR

1.

2.

3.

SEEKING  SCRIPTURE

Monday, February 3, 2025

NOTES AND REFLECTIONS **Leviticus 8-10**

Study Notes

VERSE OF THE DAY LEVITICUS 10:3

PRAYER & PRAISE

TODAY I'M GRATEFUL FOR

1.

2.

3.

SEEKING  SCRIPTURE

Tuesday, February 4, 2025

Leviticus 11-13

Study Notes

NOTES AND REFLECTIONS

VERSE OF THE DAY LEVITICUS 11:44

PRAYER & PRAISE

TODAY I'M GRATEFUL FOR

1.

2.

3.

SEEKING SCRIPTURE

Wednesday, February 5, 2025

NOTES AND REFLECTIONS   **Leviticus 14-15**

Study Notes

VERSE OF THE DAY LEVITICUS 15:31

PRAYER & PRAISE

TODAY I'M GRATEFUL FOR

1.

2.

3.

SEEKING SCRIPTURE

Thursday, February 6, 2025

Leviticus 16-18

NOTES AND REFLECTIONS

Study Notes

VERSE OF THE DAY LEVITICUS 18:4-5

PRAYER & PRAISE

TODAY I'M GRATEFUL FOR

1.

2.

3.

SEEKING SCRIPTURE

Friday, February 7, 2025

NOTES AND REFLECTIONS

Leviticus 19-21

Study Notes

VERSE OF THE DAY LEVITICUS 19:2

PRAYER & PRAISE

TODAY I'M GRATEFUL FOR

1.

2.

3.

SEEKING SCRIPTURE

Saturday, February 8, 2025

Leviticus 22-23

Study Notes

NOTES AND REFLECTIONS

VERSE OF THE DAY LEVITICUS 23:2

PRAYER & PRAISE

TODAY I'M GRATEFUL FOR

1.

2.

3.

SEEKING SCRIPTURE

Sunday, February 9, 2025

NOTES AND REFLECTIONS   **Leviticus 24-25**

Study Notes

VERSE OF THE DAY LEVITICUS 24:22

PRAYER & PRAISE

TODAY I'M GRATEFUL FOR

1.

2.

3.

SEEKING SCRIPTURE

Monday, February 10, 2025

Leviticus 26-27

Study Notes

NOTES AND REFLECTIONS

VERSE OF THE DAY LEVITICUS 26:2

PRAYER & PRAISE

TODAY I'M GRATEFUL FOR

1.

2.

3.

SEEKING SCRIPTURE

Tuesday, February 11, 2025

NOTES AND REFLECTIONS　　　　　　　　**Numbers 1-2**

Study Notes

VERSE OF THE DAY NUMBERS 1:54

PRAYER & PRAISE

TODAY I'M GRATEFUL FOR

1.

2.

3.

SEEKING SCRIPTURE

Wednesday, February 12, 2025

Numbers 3-4

Study Notes

NOTES AND REFLECTIONS

VERSE OF THE DAY NUMBERS 4:49

PRAYER & PRAISE

TODAY I'M GRATEFUL FOR

1.

2.

3.

SEEKING  SCRIPTURE

Thursday, February 13, 2025

NOTES AND REFLECTIONS

Numbers 5-6

Study Notes

VERSE OF THE DAY NUMBERS 6:24-26

PRAYER & PRAISE

TODAY I'M GRATEFUL FOR

1.

2.

3.

SEEKING SCRIPTURE

Friday, February 14, 2025

Numbers 7

Study Notes

NOTES AND REFLECTIONS

VERSE OF THE DAY NUMBERS 7:89

PRAYER & PRAISE

TODAY I'M GRATEFUL FOR

1.

2.

3.

SEEKING SCRIPTURE

Saturday, February 15, 2025

NOTES AND REFLECTIONS **Numbers 8-10**

Study Notes

VERSE OF THE DAY NUMBERS 9:14

PRAYER & PRAISE

TODAY I'M GRATEFUL FOR

1.

2.

3.

SEEKING  SCRIPTURE

Sunday, February 16, 2025

Numbers 11-13

Study Notes

NOTES AND REFLECTIONS

VERSE OF THE DAY NUMBERS 12:3

PRAYER & PRAISE

TODAY I'M GRATEFUL FOR

1.

2.

3.

SEEKING SCRIPTURE

Monday, February 17, 2025

NOTES AND REFLECTIONS **Numbers 14-15**

Study Notes

VERSE OF THE DAY NUMBERS 15:39

PRAYER & PRAISE

TODAY I'M GRATEFUL FOR

1.

2.

3.

SEEKING SCRIPTURE

Tuesday, February 18, 2025

Numbers 16-17

Study Notes

NOTES AND REFLECTIONS

VERSE OF THE DAY NUMBERS 17:10

PRAYER & PRAISE

TODAY I'M GRATEFUL FOR

1.

2.

3.

SEEKING  SCRIPTURE

Wednesday, February 19, 2025

NOTES AND REFLECTIONS　　　　　　　　　**Numbers 18-20**

Study Notes

VERSE OF THE DAY NUMBERS 18:6

PRAYER & PRAISE

TODAY I'M GRATEFUL FOR

1.

2.

3.

SEEKING SCRIPTURE

Thursday, February 20, 2025

Numbers 21-22

Study Notes

NOTES AND REFLECTIONS

VERSE OF THE DAY NUMBERS 21:16

PRAYER & PRAISE

TODAY I'M GRATEFUL FOR

1.

2.

3.

SEEKING  SCRIPTURE

Friday, February 21, 2025

NOTES AND REFLECTIONS   **Numbers 23-25**

Study Notes

VERSE OF THE DAY NUMBERS 23:19

PRAYER & PRAISE

TODAY I'M GRATEFUL FOR

1.

2.

3.

SEEKING SCRIPTURE

Saturday, February 22, 2025

Numbers 26-27

Study Notes

NOTES AND REFLECTIONS

VERSE OF THE DAY NUMBERS 27:12

PRAYER & PRAISE

TODAY I'M GRATEFUL FOR

1.

2.

3.

SEEKING SCRIPTURE

Sunday, February 23, 2025

NOTES AND REFLECTIONS **Numbers 28-30**

Study Notes

VERSE OF THE DAY NUMBERS 28:2

PRAYER & PRAISE

TODAY I'M GRATEFUL FOR

1.

2.

3.

SEEKING SCRIPTURE

Monday, February 24, 2025

Numbers 31-32

NOTES AND REFLECTIONS

Study Notes

VERSE OF THE DAY NUMBERS 32:13

PRAYER & PRAISE

TODAY I'M GRATEFUL FOR

1.

2.

3.

SEEKING SCRIPTURE

Tuesday, February 25, 2025

NOTES AND REFLECTIONS **Numbers 33-34**

Study Notes

VERSE OF THE DAY NUMBERS 33:55

PRAYER & PRAISE

TODAY I'M GRATEFUL FOR

1.

2.

3.

SEEKING  SCRIPTURE

Wednesday, February 26, 2025

Numbers 35-36

Study Notes

NOTES AND REFLECTIONS

VERSE OF THE DAY NUMBERS 35:2

TODAY I'M GRATEFUL FOR

1.

2.

3.

PRAYER & PRAISE

SEEKING  SCRIPTURE

Thursday, February 27, 2025

NOTES AND REFLECTIONS **Deuteronomy 1-2**

Study Notes

VERSE OF THE DAY DEUTERONOMY 2:7

PRAYER & PRAISE

TODAY I'M GRATEFUL FOR

1.

2.

3.

SEEKING SCRIPTURE

Friday, February 28, 2025

Deuteronomy 3-4

Study Notes

NOTES AND REFLECTIONS

VERSE OF THE DAY DEUTERONOMY 4:39

PRAYER & PRAISE

TODAY I'M GRATEFUL FOR

1.

2.

3.

SEEKING  SCRIPTURE

Saturday, March 1, 2025

NOTES AND REFLECTIONS   **Deuteronomy 5-7**

Study Notes

VERSE OF THE DAY DEUTERONOMY 6:4-6

PRAYER & PRAISE

TODAY I'M GRATEFUL FOR

1.

2.

3.

SEEKING SCRIPTURE

Sunday, March 2, 2025

Deuteronomy 8-10

NOTES AND REFLECTIONS

Study Notes

VERSE OF THE DAY DEUTERONOMY 8:6

PRAYER & PRAISE

TODAY I'M GRATEFUL FOR

1.

2.

3.

SEEKING SCRIPTURE

Monday, March 3, 2025

NOTES AND REFLECTIONS

Deuteronomy 11-13

Study Notes

VERSE OF THE DAY DEUTERONOMY 13:3

PRAYER & PRAISE

TODAY I'M GRATEFUL FOR

1.

2.

3.

SEEKING SCRIPTURE

Tuesday, March 4, 2025

Deuteronomy 14-16

NOTES AND REFLECTIONS

Study Notes

VERSE OF THE DAY DEUTERONOMY 14:2

PRAYER & PRAISE

TODAY I'M GRATEFUL FOR

1.

2.

3.

SEEKING SCRIPTURE

Wednesday, March 5, 2025

NOTES AND REFLECTIONS **Deuteronomy 17-20**

Study Notes

VERSE OF THE DAY DEUTERONOMY 18:2

PRAYER & PRAISE

TODAY I'M GRATEFUL FOR

1.

2.

3.

SEEKING SCRIPTURE

Thursday, March 6, 2025

Deuteronomy 21-23

Study Notes

NOTES AND REFLECTIONS

VERSE OF THE DAY DEUTERONOMY 21:8

PRAYER & PRAISE

TODAY I'M GRATEFUL FOR

1.

2.

3.

SEEKING SCRIPTURE

Friday, March 7, 2025

NOTES AND REFLECTIONS **Deuteronomy 24-27**

Study Notes

VERSE OF THE DAY DEUTERONOMY 24:19

PRAYER & PRAISE

TODAY I'M GRATEFUL FOR

1.

2.

3.

SEEKING SCRIPTURE

Saturday, March 8, 2025

Deuteronomy 28-29

NOTES AND REFLECTIONS

Study Notes

VERSE OF THE DAY DEUTERONOMY 29:29

PRAYER & PRAISE

TODAY I'M GRATEFUL FOR

1.

2.

3.

SEEKING  SCRIPTURE

Sunday, March 9, 2025

NOTES AND REFLECTIONS **Deuteronomy 30-31**

Study Notes

VERSE OF THE DAY DEUTERONOMY 30:11

PRAYER & PRAISE

TODAY I'M GRATEFUL FOR

1.

2.

3.

SEEKING  SCRIPTURE

Monday, March 10, 2025

Deuteronomy 32-34

NOTES AND REFLECTIONS

Study Notes

VERSE OF THE DAY DEUTERONOMY 32:4

PRAYER & PRAISE

TODAY I'M GRATEFUL FOR

1.

2.

3.

SEEKING SCRIPTURE

Tuesday, March 11, 2025

NOTES AND REFLECTIONS

Joshua 1-4

Study Notes

VERSE OF THE DAY JOSHUA 1:8

PRAYER & PRAISE

TODAY I'M GRATEFUL FOR

1.

2.

3.

SEEKING SCRIPTURE

Wednesday, March 12, 2025

Joshua 5-8

Study Notes

NOTES AND REFLECTIONS

VERSE OF THE DAY JOSHUA 6:20

PRAYER & PRAISE

TODAY I'M GRATEFUL FOR

1.

2.

3.

SEEKING SCRIPTURE

Thursday, March 13, 2025

NOTES AND REFLECTIONS

Joshua 9-11

Study Notes

VERSE OF THE DAY JOSHUA 10:13

PRAYER & PRAISE

TODAY I'M GRATEFUL FOR

1.

2.

3.

SEEKING SCRIPTURE

Friday, March 14, 2025

Joshua 12-15

NOTES AND REFLECTIONS

Study Notes

VERSE OF THE DAY JOSHUA 14:9

PRAYER & PRAISE

TODAY I'M GRATEFUL FOR

1.

2.

3.

SEEKING SCRIPTURE

Saturday, March 15, 2025

NOTES AND REFLECTIONS   Joshua 16-18

Study Notes

VERSE OF THE DAY JOSHUA 17:13

PRAYER & PRAISE

TODAY I'M GRATEFUL FOR

1.

2.

3.

SEEKING  SCRIPTURE

Sunday, March 16, 2025

Joshua 19-21

Study Notes

NOTES AND REFLECTIONS

VERSE OF THE DAY JOSHUA 21:44

PRAYER & PRAISE

TODAY I'M GRATEFUL FOR

1.

2.

3.

SEEKING SCRIPTURE

Monday, March 17, 2025

NOTES AND REFLECTIONS

Joshua 22-24

Study Notes

VERSE OF THE DAY JOSHUA 24:15

PRAYER & PRAISE

TODAY I'M GRATEFUL FOR

1.

2.

3.

SEEKING  SCRIPTURE

Tuesday, March 18, 2025

Judges 1-2

Study Notes

NOTES AND REFLECTIONS

VERSE OF THE DAY JUDGES 2:10

TODAY I'M GRATEFUL FOR

1.

2.

3.

PRAYER & PRAISE

SEEKING SCRIPTURE

Wednesday, March 19, 2025

NOTES AND REFLECTIONS **Judges 3-5**

Study Notes

VERSE OF THE DAY JUDGES 3:7

PRAYER & PRAISE

TODAY I'M GRATEFUL FOR

1.

2.

3.

SEEKING SCRIPTURE

Thursday, March 20, 2025

Judges 6-7

NOTES AND REFLECTIONS

Study Notes

VERSE OF THE DAY JUDGES 6:22

PRAYER & PRAISE

TODAY I'M GRATEFUL FOR

1.

2.

3.

SEEKING SCRIPTURE

Friday, March 21, 2025

NOTES AND REFLECTIONS

Judges 8-9

Study Notes

VERSE OF THE DAY JUDGES 8:23

PRAYER & PRAISE

TODAY I'M GRATEFUL FOR

1.

2.

3.

SEEKING  SCRIPTURE

Saturday, March 22, 2025

Judges 10-12

NOTES AND REFLECTIONS

Study Notes

VERSE OF THE DAY JUDGES 10:16

PRAYER & PRAISE

TODAY I'M GRATEFUL FOR

1.

2.

3.

SEEKING SCRIPTURE

Sunday, March 23, 2025

NOTES AND REFLECTIONS　　　　　　　　　　　**Judges 13-15**

Study Notes

VERSE OF THE DAY JUDGES 13:18

PRAYER & PRAISE

TODAY I'M GRATEFUL FOR

1.

2.

3.

SEEKING SCRIPTURE

Monday, March 24, 2025

Judges 16-18

Study Notes

NOTES AND REFLECTIONS

VERSE OF THE DAY JUDGES 16:19

PRAYER & PRAISE

TODAY I'M GRATEFUL FOR

1.

2.

3.

SEEKING SCRIPTURE

Tuesday, March 25, 2025

NOTES AND REFLECTIONS **Judges 19-21**

Study Notes

VERSE OF THE DAY JUDGES 21:25

PRAYER & PRAISE

TODAY I'M GRATEFUL FOR

1.

2.

3.

SEEKING SCRIPTURE

Wednesday, March 26, 2025

Ruth 1-4

Study Notes

NOTES AND REFLECTIONS

VERSE OF THE DAY RUTH 1:16

PRAYER & PRAISE

TODAY I'M GRATEFUL FOR

1.

2.

3.

SEEKING SCRIPTURE

Thursday, March 27, 2025

NOTES AND REFLECTIONS

1 Samuel 1-3

Study Notes

VERSE OF THE DAY 1 SAMUEL 2:2

PRAYER & PRAISE

TODAY I'M GRATEFUL FOR

1.

2.

3.

SEEKING SCRIPTURE

Friday, March 28, 2025

1 Samuel 4-8

NOTES AND REFLECTIONS

Study Notes

VERSE OF THE DAY 1 SAMUEL 8:7

PRAYER & PRAISE

TODAY I'M GRATEFUL FOR

1.

2.

3.

SEEKING SCRIPTURE

Saturday, March 29, 2025

NOTES AND REFLECTIONS **1 Samuel 9-12**

Study Notes

VERSE OF THE DAY 1 SAMUEL 12:21

PRAYER & PRAISE

TODAY I'M GRATEFUL FOR

1.

2.

3.

SEEKING SCRIPTURE

Sunday, March 30, 2025

1 Samuel 13-14

Study Notes

NOTES AND REFLECTIONS

VERSE OF THE DAY 1 SAMUEL 13:14

PRAYER & PRAISE

TODAY I'M GRATEFUL FOR

1.

2.

3.

SEEKING  SCRIPTURE

Monday, March 31, 2025

NOTES AND REFLECTIONS   **1 Samuel 15-17**

Study Notes

VERSE OF THE DAY 1 SAMUEL 15:22

PRAYER & PRAISE

TODAY I'M GRATEFUL FOR

1.

2.

3.

SEEKING SCRIPTURE

Tuesday, April 1, 2025

1 Samuel 18-20

NOTES AND REFLECTIONS

Study Notes

VERSE OF THE DAY 1 SAMUEL 18:14

PRAYER & PRAISE

TODAY I'M GRATEFUL FOR

1.

2.

3.

SEEKING SCRIPTURE

Wednesday, April 2, 2025

NOTES AND REFLECTIONS　　　　　　　　　1 Samuel 21-24

Study Notes

VERSE OF THE DAY 1 SAMUEL 24:12

PRAYER & PRAISE

TODAY I'M GRATEFUL FOR

1.

2.

3.

SEEKING SCRIPTURE

Thursday, April 3, 2025

1 Samuel 25-27

NOTES AND REFLECTIONS

Study Notes

VERSE OF THE DAY 1 SAMUEL 25:33

PRAYER & PRAISE

TODAY I'M GRATEFUL FOR

1.

2.

3.

SEEKING SCRIPTURE

Friday, April 4, 2025

NOTES AND REFLECTIONS

1 Samuel 28-31

Study Notes

VERSE OF THE DAY 1 SAMUEL 30:23

PRAYER & PRAISE

TODAY I'M GRATEFUL FOR

1.

2.

3.

SEEKING SCRIPTURE

Saturday, April 5, 2025

2 Samuel 1-3

Study Notes

NOTES AND REFLECTIONS

VERSE OF THE DAY 2 SAMUEL 2:7

PRAYER & PRAISE

TODAY I'M GRATEFUL FOR

1.

2.

3.

SEEKING SCRIPTURE

Sunday, April 6, 2025

NOTES AND REFLECTIONS　　　　　　　　　　**2 Samuel 4-7**

Study Notes

VERSE OF THE DAY 2 SAMUEL 5:10

PRAYER & PRAISE

TODAY I'M GRATEFUL FOR

1.

2.

3.

SEEKING SCRIPTURE

Monday, April 7, 2025

2 Samuel 8-12

NOTES AND REFLECTIONS

Study Notes

VERSE OF THE DAY 2 SAMUEL 12:5

PRAYER & PRAISE

TODAY I'M GRATEFUL FOR

1.

2.

3.

SEEKING SCRIPTURE

Tuesday, April 8, 2025

NOTES AND REFLECTIONS

2 Samuel 13-15

Study Notes

VERSE OF THE DAY 2 SAMUEL 15:25

PRAYER & PRAISE

TODAY I'M GRATEFUL FOR

1.

2.

3.

SEEKING SCRIPTURE

Wednesday, April 9, 2025

2 Samuel 16-18

NOTES AND REFLECTIONS

Study Notes

VERSE OF THE DAY 2 SAMUEL 18:9

PRAYER & PRAISE

TODAY I'M GRATEFUL FOR

1.

2.

3.

SEEKING SCRIPTURE

Thursday, April 10, 2025

NOTES AND REFLECTIONS 2 Samuel 19-21

Study Notes

VERSE OF THE DAY 2 SAMUEL 19:7

PRAYER & PRAISE

TODAY I'M GRATEFUL FOR

1.

2.

3.

SEEKING SCRIPTURE

Friday, April 11, 2025

2 Samuel 22-24

NOTES AND REFLECTIONS

Study Notes

VERSE OF THE DAY 2 SAMUEL 22:31- 32

PRAYER & PRAISE

TODAY I'M GRATEFUL FOR

1.

2.

3.

SEEKING SCRIPTURE

Saturday, April 12, 2025

NOTES AND REFLECTIONS 1 Kings 1-2

Study Notes

VERSE OF THE DAY 1 KINGS 2:2

PRAYER & PRAISE

TODAY I'M GRATEFUL FOR

1.

2.

3.

SEEKING  SCRIPTURE

Sunday, April 13, 2025

1 Kings 3-5

Study Notes

NOTES AND REFLECTIONS

VERSE OF THE DAY 1 KINGS 3:9

PRAYER & PRAISE

TODAY I'M GRATEFUL FOR

1.

2.

3.

SEEKING  SCRIPTURE

Monday, April 14, 2025

NOTES AND REFLECTIONS

1 Kings 6-7

Study Notes

VERSE OF THE DAY 1 KINGS 6:12-13

PRAYER & PRAISE

TODAY I'M GRATEFUL FOR

1.

2.

3.

SEEKING SCRIPTURE

Tuesday, April 15, 2025

1 Kings 8-9

Study Notes

NOTES AND REFLECTIONS

VERSE OF THE DAY 1 KINGS 8:61

PRAYER & PRAISE

TODAY I'M GRATEFUL FOR

1.

2.

3.

SEEKING SCRIPTURE

Wednesday, April 16, 2025

NOTES AND REFLECTIONS 1 Kings 10-11

Study Notes

VERSE OF THE DAY 1 KINGS 11:4

PRAYER & PRAISE

TODAY I'M GRATEFUL FOR

1.

2.

3.

SEEKING SCRIPTURE

Thursday, April 17, 2025

1 Kings 12-14

Study Notes

NOTES AND REFLECTIONS

VERSE OF THE DAY 1 KINGS 14:15

PRAYER & PRAISE

TODAY I'M GRATEFUL FOR

1.

2.

3.

SEEKING SCRIPTURE

Friday, April 18, 2025

NOTES AND REFLECTIONS 1 Kings 15-17

Study Notes

VERSE OF THE DAY 1 KINGS 17:1

PRAYER & PRAISE

TODAY I'M GRATEFUL FOR

1.

2.

3.

SEEKING SCRIPTURE

Saturday, April 19, 2025

1 Kings 18-20

Study Notes

NOTES AND REFLECTIONS

VERSE OF THE DAY 1 KINGS 19:12

TODAY I'M GRATEFUL FOR

1.

2.

3.

PRAYER & PRAISE

SEEKING SCRIPTURE

Sunday, April 20, 2025

NOTES AND REFLECTIONS　　　　　　　　　　**1 Kings 21-22**

Study Notes

VERSE OF THE DAY 1 KINGS 22:17

PRAYER & PRAISE

TODAY I'M GRATEFUL FOR

1.

2.

3.

SEEKING SCRIPTURE

Monday, April 21, 2025

2 Kings 1-3

NOTES AND REFLECTIONS

Study Notes

VERSE OF THE DAY 2 KINGS 2:10

PRAYER & PRAISE

TODAY I'M GRATEFUL FOR

1.

2.

3.

SEEKING SCRIPTURE

Tuesday, April 22, 2025

NOTES AND REFLECTIONS **2 Kings 4-5**

Study Notes

VERSE OF THE DAY 2 KINGS 4:6

PRAYER & PRAISE

TODAY I'M GRATEFUL FOR

1.

2.

3.

SEEKING SCRIPTURE

Wednesday, April 23, 2025

2 Kings 6-8

NOTES AND REFLECTIONS

Study Notes

VERSE OF THE DAY 2 KINGS 6:16

PRAYER & PRAISE

TODAY I'M GRATEFUL FOR

1.

2.

3.

SEEKING SCRIPTURE

Thursday, April 24, 2025

NOTES AND REFLECTIONS

2 Kings 9-11

Study Notes

VERSE OF THE DAY 2 KINGS 10:31

PRAYER & PRAISE

TODAY I'M GRATEFUL FOR

1.

2.

3.

SEEKING  SCRIPTURE

Friday, April 25, 2025

2 Kings 12-14

Study Notes

NOTES AND REFLECTIONS

VERSE OF THE DAY 2 KINGS 13:21

PRAYER & PRAISE

TODAY I'M GRATEFUL FOR

1.

2.

3.

SEEKING SCRIPTURE

Saturday, April 26, 2025

NOTES AND REFLECTIONS

2 Kings 15-17

Study Notes

VERSE OF THE DAY 2 KINGS 17:13

PRAYER & PRAISE

TODAY I'M GRATEFUL FOR

1.

2.

3.

SEEKING SCRIPTURE

Sunday, April 27, 2025

2 Kings 18-19

NOTES AND REFLECTIONS

Study Notes

VERSE OF THE DAY 2 KINGS 18:6-7

PRAYER & PRAISE

TODAY I'M GRATEFUL FOR

1.

2.

3.

SEEKING SCRIPTURE

Monday, April 28, 2025

NOTES AND REFLECTIONS **2 Kings 20-22**

Study Notes

VERSE OF THE DAY 2 KINGS 20:9-10

PRAYER & PRAISE

TODAY I'M GRATEFUL FOR

1.

2.

3.

SEEKING SCRIPTURE

Tuesday, April 29, 2025

2 Kings 23-25

NOTES AND REFLECTIONS

Study Notes

VERSE OF THE DAY 2 KINGS 23:3

PRAYER & PRAISE

TODAY I'M GRATEFUL FOR

1.

2.

3.

SEEKING SCRIPTURE

Wednesday, April 30, 2025

NOTES AND REFLECTIONS 1 Chronicles 1-2

Study Notes

VERSE OF THE DAY 1 CHRONICLES 2:1-2

PRAYER & PRAISE

TODAY I'M GRATEFUL FOR

1.

2.

3.

SEEKING SCRIPTURE

Thursday, May 1, 2025

1 Chronicles 3-5

Study Notes

NOTES AND REFLECTIONS

VERSE OF THE DAY 1 CHRONICLES 4:10

TODAY I'M GRATEFUL FOR

1.

2.

3.

PRAYER & PRAISE

SEEKING SCRIPTURE

Friday, May 2, 2025

NOTES AND REFLECTIONS

1 Chronicles 6

Study Notes

VERSE OF THE DAY 1 CHRONICLES 6:49

PRAYER & PRAISE

TODAY I'M GRATEFUL FOR

1.

2.

3.

SEEKING SCRIPTURE

Saturday, May 3, 2025

1 Chronicles 7-8

NOTES AND REFLECTIONS

Study Notes

VERSE OF THE DAY 1 CHRONICLES 8:33

TODAY I'M GRATEFUL FOR

1.

2.

3.

PRAYER & PRAISE

SEEKING SCRIPTURE

Sunday, May 4, 2025

NOTES AND REFLECTIONS

1 Chronicles 9-11

Study Notes

VERSE OF THE DAY 1 CHRONICLES 11:14

PRAYER & PRAISE

TODAY I'M GRATEFUL FOR

1.

2.

3.

SEEKING SCRIPTURE

Monday, May 5, 2025

1 Chronicles 12-14

Study Notes

NOTES AND REFLECTIONS

VERSE OF THE DAY 1 CHRONICLES 12:18

PRAYER & PRAISE

TODAY I'M GRATEFUL FOR

1.

2.

3.

SEEKING SCRIPTURE

Tuesday, May 6, 2025

NOTES AND REFLECTIONS **1 Chronicles 15-17**

Study Notes

VERSE OF THE DAY 1 CHRONICLES 16:9

PRAYER & PRAISE

TODAY I'M GRATEFUL FOR

1.

2.

3.

SEEKING SCRIPTURE

Wednesday, May 7, 2025

1 Chronicles 18-21

NOTES AND REFLECTIONS

Study Notes

VERSE OF THE DAY 1 CHRONICLES 21:8

TODAY I'M GRATEFUL FOR

1.

2.

3.

PRAYER & PRAISE

SEEKING SCRIPTURE

Thursday, May 8, 2025

NOTES AND REFLECTIONS 1 Chronicles 22-24

Study Notes

VERSE OF THE DAY 1 CHRONICLES 22:12-13

PRAYER & PRAISE

TODAY I'M GRATEFUL FOR

1.

2.

3.

SEEKING SCRIPTURE

Friday, May 9, 2025

1 Chronicles 25-27

Study Notes

NOTES AND REFLECTIONS

VERSE OF THE DAY 1 CHRONICLES 27:23

PRAYER & PRAISE

TODAY I'M GRATEFUL FOR

1.

2.

3.

SEEKING SCRIPTURE

Saturday, May 10, 2025

NOTES AND REFLECTIONS **1 Chron 28-2 Chron 1**

Study Notes

VERSE OF THE DAY 1 CHRONICLES 28:9

PRAYER & PRAISE

TODAY I'M GRATEFUL FOR

1.

2.

3.

SEEKING  SCRIPTURE

Sunday, May 11, 2025

2 Chronicles 2-5

Study Notes

NOTES AND REFLECTIONS

VERSE OF THE DAY 2 CHRONICLES 5:13

PRAYER & PRAISE

TODAY I'M GRATEFUL FOR

1.

2.

3.

SEEKING SCRIPTURE

Monday, May 12, 2025

NOTES AND REFLECTIONS

2 Chronicles 6-8

Study Notes

VERSE OF THE DAY 2 CHRONICLES 7:14

PRAYER & PRAISE

TODAY I'M GRATEFUL FOR

1.

2.

3.

SEEKING SCRIPTURE

Tuesday, May 13, 2025

2 Chronicles 9-12

Study Notes

NOTES AND REFLECTIONS

VERSE OF THE DAY 2 CHRONICLES 10:8

TODAY I'M GRATEFUL FOR

1.

2.

3.

PRAYER & PRAISE

SEEKING SCRIPTURE

Wednesday, May 14, 2025

NOTES AND REFLECTIONS

2 Chronicles 13-17

Study Notes

VERSE OF THE DAY 2 CHRONICLES 14:11

PRAYER & PRAISE

TODAY I'M GRATEFUL FOR

1.

2.

3.

SEEKING SCRIPTURE

Thursday, May 15, 2025

2 Chronicles 18-20

NOTES AND REFLECTIONS

Study Notes

VERSE OF THE DAY 2 CHRONICLES 20:15

PRAYER & PRAISE

TODAY I'M GRATEFUL FOR

1.

2.

3.

SEEKING SCRIPTURE

Friday, May 16, 2025

NOTES AND REFLECTIONS

2 Chronicles 21-24

Study Notes

VERSE OF THE DAY 2 CHRONICLES 24:8

PRAYER & PRAISE

TODAY I'M GRATEFUL FOR

1.

2.

3.

SEEKING SCRIPTURE

Saturday, May 17, 2025

2 Chronicles 25-27

NOTES AND REFLECTIONS

Study Notes

VERSE OF THE DAY 2 CHRONICLES 25:2

PRAYER & PRAISE

TODAY I'M GRATEFUL FOR

1.

2.

3.

SEEKING SCRIPTURE

Sunday, May 18, 2025

NOTES AND REFLECTIONS

2 Chronicles 28-31

Study Notes

VERSE OF THE DAY 2 CHRONICLES 31:1

PRAYER & PRAISE

TODAY I'M GRATEFUL FOR

1.

2.

3.

SEEKING SCRIPTURE

Monday, May 19, 2025

2 Chronicles 32-34

NOTES AND REFLECTIONS

Study Notes

VERSE OF THE DAY 2 CHRONICLES 34:31

TODAY I'M GRATEFUL FOR

1.

2.

3.

PRAYER & PRAISE

SEEKING SCRIPTURE

Tuesday, May 20, 2025

NOTES AND REFLECTIONS　　　　　　　　**2 Chronicles 35-36**

Study Notes

VERSE OF THE DAY 2 CHRONICLES 35:16

PRAYER & PRAISE

TODAY I'M GRATEFUL FOR

1.

2.

3.

SEEKING SCRIPTURE

Wednesday, May 21, 2025

Ezra 1-3

NOTES AND REFLECTIONS

Study Notes

VERSE OF THE DAY EZRA 3:6

PRAYER & PRAISE

TODAY I'M GRATEFUL FOR

1.

2.

3.

SEEKING SCRIPTURE

Thursday, May 22, 2025

NOTES AND REFLECTIONS

Ezra 4-7

Study Notes

VERSE OF THE DAY EZRA 7:10

PRAYER & PRAISE

TODAY I'M GRATEFUL FOR

1.

2.

3.

SEEKING SCRIPTURE

Friday, May 23, 2025

Ezra 8-10

NOTES AND REFLECTIONS

Study Notes

VERSE OF THE DAY EZRA 9:15

PRAYER & PRAISE

TODAY I'M GRATEFUL FOR

1.

2.

3.

SEEKING SCRIPTURE

Saturday, May 24, 2025

NOTES AND REFLECTIONS Nehemiah 1-3

Study Notes

VERSE OF THE DAY NEHEMIAH 1:7

PRAYER & PRAISE

TODAY I'M GRATEFUL FOR

1.

2.

3.

SEEKING  SCRIPTURE

Sunday, May 25, 2025

Nehemiah 4-6

NOTES AND REFLECTIONS

Study Notes

VERSE OF THE DAY NEHEMIAH 4:14

PRAYER & PRAISE

TODAY I'M GRATEFUL FOR

1.

2.

3.

SEEKING SCRIPTURE

Monday, May 26, 2025

NOTES AND REFLECTIONS   Nehemiah 7

Study Notes

VERSE OF THE DAY NEHEMIAH 7:2

PRAYER & PRAISE

TODAY I'M GRATEFUL FOR

1.

2.

3.

SEEKING  SCRIPTURE

Tuesday, May 27, 2025

Nehemiah 8-9

NOTES AND REFLECTIONS

Study Notes

VERSE OF THE DAY NEHEMIAH 8:10

PRAYER & PRAISE

TODAY I'M GRATEFUL FOR

1.

2.

3.

SEEKING SCRIPTURE

Wednesday, May 28, 2025

NOTES AND REFLECTIONS Nehemiah 10-11

Study Notes

VERSE OF THE DAY NEHEMIAH 11:2

PRAYER & PRAISE

TODAY I'M GRATEFUL FOR

1.

2.

3.

SEEKING SCRIPTURE

Thursday, May 29, 2025

Nehemiah 12-13

Study Notes

NOTES AND REFLECTIONS

VERSE OF THE DAY NEHEMIAH 12:43

PRAYER & PRAISE

TODAY I'M GRATEFUL FOR

1.

2.

3.

SEEKING SCRIPTURE

Friday, May 30, 2025

NOTES AND REFLECTIONS   Esther 1-5

Study Notes

VERSE OF THE DAY ESTHER 4:14

PRAYER & PRAISE

TODAY I'M GRATEFUL FOR

1.

2.

3.

SEEKING SCRIPTURE

Saturday, May 31, 2025

Esther 6-10

Study Notes

NOTES AND REFLECTIONS

VERSE OF THE DAY ESTHER 9:2

PRAYER & PRAISE

TODAY I'M GRATEFUL FOR

1.

2.

3.

SEEKING SCRIPTURE

Sunday, June 1, 2025

NOTES AND REFLECTIONS **Job 1-4**

Study Notes

VERSE OF THE DAY JOB 1:20-21

PRAYER & PRAISE

TODAY I'M GRATEFUL FOR

1.

2.

3.

SEEKING  SCRIPTURE

Monday, June 2, 2025

Job 5-7

NOTES AND REFLECTIONS

Study Notes

VERSE OF THE DAY JOB 5:17

PRAYER & PRAISE

TODAY I'M GRATEFUL FOR

1.

2.

3.

SEEKING SCRIPTURE

Tuesday, June 3, 2025

NOTES AND REFLECTIONS **Job 8-10**

Study Notes

VERSE OF THE DAY JOB 9:8-9

PRAYER & PRAISE

TODAY I'M GRATEFUL FOR

1.

2.

3.

SEEKING SCRIPTURE

Wednesday, June 4, 2025

Job 11-13

Study Notes

NOTES AND REFLECTIONS

VERSE OF THE DAY JOB 13:15

PRAYER & PRAISE

TODAY I'M GRATEFUL FOR

1.

2.

3.

SEEKING SCRIPTURE

Thursday, June 5, 2025

NOTES AND REFLECTIONS

Job 14-16

Study Notes

VERSE OF THE DAY JOB 15:31

PRAYER & PRAISE

TODAY I'M GRATEFUL FOR

1.

2.

3.

SEEKING SCRIPTURE

Friday, June 6, 2025

Job 17-20

NOTES AND REFLECTIONS

Study Notes

VERSE OF THE DAY JOB 19:25

PRAYER & PRAISE

TODAY I'M GRATEFUL FOR

1.

2.

3.

SEEKING SCRIPTURE

Saturday, June 7, 2025

NOTES AND REFLECTIONS　　　　　　　　　　　　　　**Job 21-23**

Study Notes

VERSE OF THE DAY JOB 23:12

PRAYER & PRAISE

TODAY I'M GRATEFUL FOR

1.

2.

3.

SEEKING SCRIPTURE

Sunday, June 8, 2025

Job 24-28

Study Notes

NOTES AND REFLECTIONS

VERSE OF THE DAY JOB 28:28

PRAYER & PRAISE

TODAY I'M GRATEFUL FOR

1.

2.

3.

SEEKING SCRIPTURE

Monday, June 9, 2025

NOTES AND REFLECTIONS **Job 29-31**

Study Notes

VERSE OF THE DAY JOB 29:4

PRAYER & PRAISE

TODAY I'M GRATEFUL FOR

1.

2.

3.

SEEKING SCRIPTURE

Tuesday, June 10, 2025

Job 32-34

Study Notes

NOTES AND REFLECTIONS

VERSE OF THE DAY JOB 34:3-4

PRAYER & PRAISE

TODAY I'M GRATEFUL FOR

1.

2.

3.

SEEKING SCRIPTURE

Wednesday, June 11, 2025

NOTES AND REFLECTIONS **Job 35-37**

Study Notes

VERSE OF THE DAY JOB 36:10

PRAYER & PRAISE

TODAY I'M GRATEFUL FOR

1.

2.

3.

SEEKING SCRIPTURE

Thursday, June 12, 2025

Job 38-39

NOTES AND REFLECTIONS

Study Notes

VERSE OF THE DAY JOB 40:6-7

PRAYER & PRAISE

TODAY I'M GRATEFUL FOR

1.

2.

3.

SEEKING SCRIPTURE

Friday, June 13, 2025

NOTES AND REFLECTIONS

Job 40-42

Study Notes

VERSE OF THE DAY JOB 42:10

PRAYER & PRAISE

TODAY I'M GRATEFUL FOR

1.

2.

3.

SEEKING SCRIPTURE

Saturday, June 14, 2025

Psalm 1-8

Study Notes

NOTES AND REFLECTIONS

VERSE OF THE DAY PSALM 1:1

PRAYER & PRAISE

TODAY I'M GRATEFUL FOR

1.

2.

3.

SEEKING SCRIPTURE

Sunday, June 15, 2025

NOTES AND REFLECTIONS Psalm 9-16

Study Notes

VERSE OF THE DAY PSALM 9:1

PRAYER & PRAISE

TODAY I'M GRATEFUL FOR

1.

2.

3.

SEEKING SCRIPTURE

Monday, June 16, 2025

Psalm 17-20

NOTES AND REFLECTIONS

Study Notes

VERSE OF THE DAY PSALM 19:7

TODAY I'M GRATEFUL FOR

1.

2.

3.

PRAYER & PRAISE

SEEKING SCRIPTURE

Tuesday, June 17, 2025

NOTES AND REFLECTIONS Psalm 21-25

Study Notes

VERSE OF THE DAY PSALM 25:4-5

PRAYER & PRAISE

TODAY I'M GRATEFUL FOR

1.

2.

3.

SEEKING SCRIPTURE

Wednesday, June 18, 2025

Psalm 26-31

Study Notes

NOTES AND REFLECTIONS

VERSE OF THE DAY PSALM 26:1-2

PRAYER & PRAISE

TODAY I'M GRATEFUL FOR

1.

2.

3.

SEEKING SCRIPTURE

Thursday, June 19, 2025

NOTES AND REFLECTIONS　　　　　　　　　　　　　**Psalm 32-35**

Study Notes

VERSE OF THE DAY PSALM 33:18

PRAYER & PRAISE

TODAY I'M GRATEFUL FOR

1.

2.

3.

SEEKING SCRIPTURE

Friday, June 20, 2025

Psalm 36-39

NOTES AND REFLECTIONS

Study Notes

VERSE OF THE DAY PSALM 36:7

PRAYER & PRAISE

TODAY I'M GRATEFUL FOR

1.

2.

3.

SEEKING SCRIPTURE

Saturday, June 21, 2025

NOTES AND REFLECTIONS Psalm 40-45

Study Notes

VERSE OF THE DAY PSALM 40:16

PRAYER & PRAISE

TODAY I'M GRATEFUL FOR

1.

2.

3.

SEEKING SCRIPTURE

Sunday, June 22, 2025

Psalm 46-50

NOTES AND REFLECTIONS

Study Notes

VERSE OF THE DAY PSALM 48:10

PRAYER & PRAISE

TODAY I'M GRATEFUL FOR

1.

2.

3.

SEEKING SCRIPTURE

Monday, June 23, 2025

NOTES AND REFLECTIONS

Psalm 51-57

Study Notes

VERSE OF THE DAY PSALM 56:4

PRAYER & PRAISE

TODAY I'M GRATEFUL FOR

1.

2.

3.

SEEKING SCRIPTURE

Tuesday, June 24, 2025

Psalm 58-65

NOTES AND REFLECTIONS

Study Notes

VERSE OF THE DAY PSALM 62:11-12

PRAYER & PRAISE

TODAY I'M GRATEFUL FOR

1.

2.

3.

SEEKING SCRIPTURE

Wednesday, June 25, 2025

NOTES AND REFLECTIONS — Psalm 66-69

Study Notes

VERSE OF THE DAY PSALM 66:16

PRAYER & PRAISE

TODAY I'M GRATEFUL FOR

1.

2.

3.

SEEKING SCRIPTURE

Thursday, June 26, 2025

Psalm 70-73

NOTES AND REFLECTIONS

Study Notes

VERSE OF THE DAY PSALM 71:19

PRAYER & PRAISE

TODAY I'M GRATEFUL FOR

1.

2.

3.

SEEKING SCRIPTURE

Friday, June 27, 2025

NOTES AND REFLECTIONS

Psalm 74-77

Study Notes

VERSE OF THE DAY PSALM 77:12

PRAYER & PRAISE

TODAY I'M GRATEFUL FOR

1.

2.

3.

SEEKING SCRIPTURE

Saturday, June 28, 2025

Psalm 78-79

NOTES AND REFLECTIONS

Study Notes

VERSE OF THE DAY PSALM 79:9

PRAYER & PRAISE

TODAY I'M GRATEFUL FOR

1.

2.

3.

SEEKING SCRIPTURE

Sunday, June 29, 2025

NOTES AND REFLECTIONS　　　　　　　　　　Psalm 80-85

Study Notes

VERSE OF THE DAY PSALM 81:3

PRAYER & PRAISE

TODAY I'M GRATEFUL FOR

1.

2.

3.

SEEKING SCRIPTURE

Monday, June 30, 2025

Psalm 86-89

NOTES AND REFLECTIONS

Study Notes

VERSE OF THE DAY PSALM 86:11

PRAYER & PRAISE

TODAY I'M GRATEFUL FOR

1.

2.

3.

SEEKING SCRIPTURE

Tuesday, July 1, 2025

NOTES AND REFLECTIONS   Psalm 90-95

Study Notes

VERSE OF THE DAY PSALM 91:4

PRAYER & PRAISE

TODAY I'M GRATEFUL FOR

1.

2.

3.

SEEKING SCRIPTURE

Wednesday, July 2, 2025

Psalm 96-102

Study Notes

NOTES AND REFLECTIONS

VERSE OF THE DAY PSALM 98:3

PRAYER & PRAISE

TODAY I'M GRATEFUL FOR

1.

2.

3.

SEEKING SCRIPTURE

Thursday, July 3, 2025

NOTES AND REFLECTIONS **Psalm 103-105**

Study Notes

VERSE OF THE DAY PSALM 104:33

PRAYER & PRAISE

TODAY I'M GRATEFUL FOR

1.

2.

3.

SEEKING SCRIPTURE

Friday, July 4, 2025

Psalm 106-107

Study Notes

NOTES AND REFLECTIONS

VERSE OF THE DAY PSALM 107:9

PRAYER & PRAISE

TODAY I'M GRATEFUL FOR

1.

2.

3.

SEEKING SCRIPTURE

Saturday, July 5, 2025

NOTES AND REFLECTIONS   Psalm 108-114

Study Notes

VERSE OF THE DAY PSALM 112:1

PRAYER & PRAISE

TODAY I'M GRATEFUL FOR

1.

2.

3.

SEEKING SCRIPTURE

Sunday, July 6, 2025

Psalm 115-118

NOTES AND REFLECTIONS

Study Notes

VERSE OF THE DAY PSALM 118:6

PRAYER & PRAISE

TODAY I'M GRATEFUL FOR

1.

2.

3.

SEEKING SCRIPTURE

Monday, July 7, 2025

NOTES AND REFLECTIONS Psalm 119:1-88

Study Notes

VERSE OF THE DAY PSALM 119:11

PRAYER & PRAISE

TODAY I'M GRATEFUL FOR

1.

2.

3.

SEEKING SCRIPTURE

Tuesday, July 8, 2025

Psalm 119:89-176

NOTES AND REFLECTIONS

Study Notes

VERSE OF THE DAY PSALM 119:97

PRAYER & PRAISE

TODAY I'M GRATEFUL FOR

1.

2.

3.

SEEKING SCRIPTURE

Wednesday, July 9, 2025

NOTES AND REFLECTIONS　　　　　　　　　　　　Psalm 120-132

Study Notes

VERSE OF THE DAY PSALM 125:2

PRAYER & PRAISE

TODAY I'M GRATEFUL FOR

1.

2.

3.

SEEKING SCRIPTURE

Thursday, July 10, 2025

Psalm 133-139

NOTES AND REFLECTIONS

Study Notes

VERSE OF THE DAY PSALM 133:1

PRAYER & PRAISE

TODAY I'M GRATEFUL FOR

1.

2.

3.

SEEKING SCRIPTURE

Friday, July 11, 2025

NOTES AND REFLECTIONS   Psalm 140-145

Study Notes

VERSE OF THE DAY PSALM 143:10

PRAYER & PRAISE

TODAY I'M GRATEFUL FOR

1.

2.

3.

SEEKING SCRIPTURE

Saturday, July 12, 2025

Psalm 146-150

NOTES AND REFLECTIONS

Study Notes

VERSE OF THE DAY PSALM 149:1-2

PRAYER & PRAISE

TODAY I'M GRATEFUL FOR

1.

2.

3.

SEEKING SCRIPTURE

Sunday, July 13, 2025

NOTES AND REFLECTIONS   **Proverbs 1-3**

Study Notes

VERSE OF THE DAY PROVERBS 1:7

PRAYER & PRAISE

TODAY I'M GRATEFUL FOR

1.

2.

3.

SEEKING SCRIPTURE

Monday, July 14, 2025

Proverbs 4-6

NOTES AND REFLECTIONS

Study Notes

VERSE OF THE DAY PROVERBS 6:16-19

PRAYER & PRAISE

TODAY I'M GRATEFUL FOR

1.

2.

3.

SEEKING  SCRIPTURE

Tuesday, July 15, 2025

NOTES AND REFLECTIONS   Proverbs 7-9

Study Notes

VERSE OF THE DAY PROVERBS 8:8

PRAYER & PRAISE

TODAY I'M GRATEFUL FOR

1.

2.

3.

SEEKING  SCRIPTURE

Wednesday, July 16, 2025

Proverbs 10-12

Study Notes

NOTES AND REFLECTIONS

VERSE OF THE DAY PROVERBS 10:2

PRAYER & PRAISE

TODAY I'M GRATEFUL FOR

1.

2.

3.

SEEKING SCRIPTURE

Thursday, July 17, 2025

NOTES AND REFLECTIONS **Proverbs 13-15**

Study Notes

VERSE OF THE DAY PROVERBS 13:2-3

PRAYER & PRAISE

TODAY I'M GRATEFUL FOR

1.

2.

3.

SEEKING  SCRIPTURE

Friday, July 18, 2025

Proverbs 16-18

NOTES AND REFLECTIONS

Study Notes

VERSE OF THE DAY PROVERBS 16:24

PRAYER & PRAISE

TODAY I'M GRATEFUL FOR

1.

2.

3.

SEEKING  SCRIPTURE

Saturday, July 19, 2025

NOTES AND REFLECTIONS Proverbs 19-21

Study Notes

VERSE OF THE DAY PROVERBS 19:11

PRAYER & PRAISE

TODAY I'M GRATEFUL FOR

1.

2.

3.

SEEKING  SCRIPTURE

Sunday, July 20, 2025

Proverbs 22-23

Study Notes

NOTES AND REFLECTIONS

VERSE OF THE DAY PROVERBS 22:8

TODAY I'M GRATEFUL FOR

1.

2.

3.

PRAYER & PRAISE

SEEKING  SCRIPTURE

Monday, July 21, 2025

NOTES AND REFLECTIONS

Proverbs 24-26

Study Notes

VERSE OF THE DAY PROVERBS 24:17

PRAYER & PRAISE

TODAY I'M GRATEFUL FOR

1.

2.

3.

SEEKING SCRIPTURE

Tuesday, July 22, 2025

Proverbs 27-29

Study Notes

NOTES AND REFLECTIONS

VERSE OF THE DAY PROVERBS 27:2

TODAY I'M GRATEFUL FOR

1.

2.

3.

PRAYER & PRAISE

SEEKING SCRIPTURE

Wednesday, July 23, 2025

NOTES AND REFLECTIONSProverbs 30-31

Study Notes

VERSE OF THE DAY PROVERBS 30:8

PRAYER & PRAISE

TODAY I'M GRATEFUL FOR

1.

2.

3.

SEEKING SCRIPTURE

Thursday, July 24, 2025

Ecclesiastes 1-4

NOTES AND REFLECTIONS

Study Notes

VERSE OF THE DAY ECCLESIASTES 2:13

PRAYER & PRAISE

TODAY I'M GRATEFUL FOR

1.

2.

3.

SEEKING SCRIPTURE

Friday, July 25, 2025

NOTES AND REFLECTIONS **Ecclesiastes 5-8**

Study Notes

VERSE OF THE DAY ECCLESIASTES 7:21-22

PRAYER & PRAISE

TODAY I'M GRATEFUL FOR

1.

2.

3.

SEEKING SCRIPTURE

Saturday, July 26, 2025

Ecclesiastes 9-12

Study Notes

NOTES AND REFLECTIONS

VERSE OF THE DAY ECCLESIASTES 9:17-18

TODAY I'M GRATEFUL FOR

1.

2.

3.

PRAYER & PRAISE

SEEKING SCRIPTURE

Sunday, July 27, 2025

NOTES AND REFLECTIONS   Solomon 1-8

Study Notes

VERSE OF THE DAY SOLOMON 8:6

PRAYER & PRAISE

TODAY I'M GRATEFUL FOR

1.

2.

3.

SEEKING  SCRIPTURE

Monday, July 28, 2025

Isaiah 1-4

Study Notes

NOTES AND REFLECTIONS

VERSE OF THE DAY ISAIAH 2:3

TODAY I'M GRATEFUL FOR

1.

2.

3.

PRAYER & PRAISE

SEEKING  SCRIPTURE

Tuesday, July 29, 2025

NOTES AND REFLECTIONS Isaiah 5-8

Study Notes

VERSE OF THE DAY ISAIAH 5:13

PRAYER & PRAISE

TODAY I'M GRATEFUL FOR

1.

2.

3.

SEEKING SCRIPTURE

Wednesday, July 30, 2025

Isaiah 9-12

Study Notes

NOTES AND REFLECTIONS

VERSE OF THE DAY ISAIAH 12:2

PRAYER & PRAISE

TODAY I'M GRATEFUL FOR

1.

2.

3.

SEEKING  SCRIPTURE

Thursday, July 31, 2025

NOTES AND REFLECTIONS   Isaiah 13-17

Study Notes

VERSE OF THE DAY ISAIAH 17:7

PRAYER & PRAISE

TODAY I'M GRATEFUL FOR

1.

2.

3.

SEEKING SCRIPTURE

Friday, August 1, 2025

Isaiah 18-22

NOTES AND REFLECTIONS

Study Notes

VERSE OF THE DAY ISAIAH 18:3

PRAYER & PRAISE

TODAY I'M GRATEFUL FOR

1.

2.

3.

SEEKING SCRIPTURE

Saturday, August 2, 2025

NOTES AND REFLECTIONS   **Isaiah 23-27**

Study Notes

VERSE OF THE DAY ISAIAH 26:3

PRAYER & PRAISE

TODAY I'M GRATEFUL FOR

1.

2.

3.

SEEKING  SCRIPTURE

Sunday, August 3, 2025

Isaiah 28-30

NOTES AND REFLECTIONS

Study Notes

VERSE OF THE DAY ISAIAH 29:16

PRAYER & PRAISE

TODAY I'M GRATEFUL FOR

1.

2.

3.

SEEKING SCRIPTURE

Monday, August 4, 2025

NOTES AND REFLECTIONS　　　　　　　　　　　Isaiah 31-35

Study Notes

VERSE OF THE DAY ISAIAH 32:17-18

PRAYER & PRAISE

TODAY I'M GRATEFUL FOR

1.

2.

3.

SEEKING SCRIPTURE

Tuesday, August 5, 2025

Isaiah 36-41

NOTES AND REFLECTIONS

Study Notes

VERSE OF THE DAY ISAIAH 41:10

PRAYER & PRAISE

TODAY I'M GRATEFUL FOR

1.

2.

3.

SEEKING SCRIPTURE

Wednesday, August 6, 2025

NOTES AND REFLECTIONS Isaiah 42-44

Study Notes

VERSE OF THE DAY ISAIAH 43:3

PRAYER & PRAISE

TODAY I'M GRATEFUL FOR

1.

2.

3.

SEEKING SCRIPTURE

Thursday, August 7, 2025

Isaiah 45-48

NOTES AND REFLECTIONS

Study Notes

VERSE OF THE DAY ISAIAH 48:17

PRAYER & PRAISE

TODAY I'M GRATEFUL FOR

1.

2.

3.

SEEKING SCRIPTURE

Friday, August 8, 2025

NOTES AND REFLECTIONS   Isaiah 49-53

Study Notes

VERSE OF THE DAY ISAIAH 50:4

PRAYER & PRAISE

TODAY I'M GRATEFUL FOR

1.

2.

3.

SEEKING  SCRIPTURE

Saturday, August 9, 2025

Isaiah 54-58

NOTES AND REFLECTIONS

Study Notes

VERSE OF THE DAY ISAIAH 56:7

PRAYER & PRAISE

TODAY I'M GRATEFUL FOR

1.

2.

3.

SEEKING SCRIPTURE

Sunday, August 10, 2025

NOTES AND REFLECTIONS   **Isaiah 59-63**

Study Notes

VERSE OF THE DAY ISAIAH 63:15

PRAYER & PRAISE

TODAY I'M GRATEFUL FOR

1.

2.

3.

SEEKING SCRIPTURE

Monday, August 11, 2025

Isaiah 64-66

Study Notes

NOTES AND REFLECTIONS

VERSE OF THE DAY ISAIAH 65:2

TODAY I'M GRATEFUL FOR

1.

2.

3.

PRAYER & PRAISE

SEEKING  SCRIPTURE

Tuesday, August 12, 2025

NOTES AND REFLECTIONS   **Jeremiah 1-3**

Study Notes

VERSE OF THE DAY JEREMIAH 2:17

PRAYER & PRAISE

TODAY I'M GRATEFUL FOR

1.

2.

3.

SEEKING SCRIPTURE

Wednesday, August 13, 2025

Jeremiah 4-6

NOTES AND REFLECTIONS

Study Notes

VERSE OF THE DAY JEREMIAH 6:16

PRAYER & PRAISE

TODAY I'M GRATEFUL FOR

1.

2.

3.

SEEKING SCRIPTURE

Thursday, August 14, 2025

NOTES AND REFLECTIONS **Jeremiah 7-9**

Study Notes

VERSE OF THE DAY JEREMIAH 7:23

PRAYER & PRAISE

TODAY I'M GRATEFUL FOR

1.

2.

3.

SEEKING  SCRIPTURE

Friday, August 15, 2025

Jeremiah 10-13

NOTES AND REFLECTIONS

Study Notes

VERSE OF THE DAY JEREMIAH 11:14

PRAYER & PRAISE

TODAY I'M GRATEFUL FOR

1.

2.

3.

SEEKING  SCRIPTURE

Saturday, August 16, 2025

NOTES AND REFLECTIONS Jeremiah 14-17

Study Notes

VERSE OF THE DAY JEREMIAH 17:9-10

PRAYER & PRAISE

TODAY I'M GRATEFUL FOR

1.

2.

3.

SEEKING  SCRIPTURE

Sunday, August 17, 2025

Jeremiah 18-22

Study Notes

NOTES AND REFLECTIONS

VERSE OF THE DAY JEREMIAH 21:8

PRAYER & PRAISE

TODAY I'M GRATEFUL FOR

1.

2.

3.

SEEKING SCRIPTURE

Monday, August 18, 2025

NOTES AND REFLECTIONS

Jeremiah 23-25

Study Notes

VERSE OF THE DAY JEREMIAH 23:16

PRAYER & PRAISE

TODAY I'M GRATEFUL FOR

1.

2.

3.

SEEKING SCRIPTURE

Tuesday, August 19, 2025

Jeremiah 26-29

Study Notes

NOTES AND REFLECTIONS

VERSE OF THE DAY JEREMIAH 29:13

TODAY I'M GRATEFUL FOR

1.

2.

3.

PRAYER & PRAISE

SEEKING  SCRIPTURE

Wednesday, August 20, 2025

NOTES AND REFLECTIONS Jeremiah 30-31

Study Notes

VERSE OF THE DAY JEREMIAH 31:33

PRAYER & PRAISE

TODAY I'M GRATEFUL FOR

1.

2.

3.

SEEKING  SCRIPTURE

Thursday, August 21, 2025

Jeremiah 32-34

Study Notes

NOTES AND REFLECTIONS

VERSE OF THE DAY JEREMIAH 32:17

TODAY I'M GRATEFUL FOR

1.

2.

3.

PRAYER & PRAISE

SEEKING SCRIPTURE

Friday, August 22, 2025

NOTES AND REFLECTIONS   **Jeremiah 35-37**

Study Notes

VERSE OF THE DAY JEREMIAH 35:15

PRAYER & PRAISE

TODAY I'M GRATEFUL FOR

1.

2.

3.

SEEKING  SCRIPTURE

Saturday, August 23, 2025

Jeremiah 38-41

Study Notes

NOTES AND REFLECTIONS

VERSE OF THE DAY JEREMIAH 40:3

PRAYER & PRAISE

TODAY I'M GRATEFUL FOR

1.

2.

3.

SEEKING  SCRIPTURE

Sunday, August 24, 2025

NOTES AND REFLECTIONS **Jeremiah 42-45**

Study Notes

VERSE OF THE DAY JEREMIAH 42:2

PRAYER & PRAISE

TODAY I'M GRATEFUL FOR

1.

2.

3.

SEEKING SCRIPTURE

Monday, August 25, 2025

Jeremiah 46-48

Study Notes

NOTES AND REFLECTIONS

VERSE OF THE DAY JEREMIAH 46:27

PRAYER & PRAISE

TODAY I'M GRATEFUL FOR

1.

2.

3.

SEEKING SCRIPTURE

Tuesday, August 26, 2025

NOTES AND REFLECTIONS **Jeremiah 49-50**

Study Notes

VERSE OF THE DAY JEREMIAH 50:5

PRAYER & PRAISE

TODAY I'M GRATEFUL FOR

1.

2.

3.

SEEKING  SCRIPTURE

Wednesday, August 27, 2025

Jeremiah 51-52

NOTES AND REFLECTIONS

Study Notes

VERSE OF THE DAY JEREMIAH 51:5

PRAYER & PRAISE

TODAY I'M GRATEFUL FOR

1.

2.

3.

SEEKING  SCRIPTURE

Thursday, August 28, 2025

NOTES AND REFLECTIONS **Lamentations 1-3:36**

Study Notes

VERSE OF THE DAY LAMENTATIONS 3:21-23

PRAYER & PRAISE

TODAY I'M GRATEFUL FOR

1.

2.

3.

SEEKING SCRIPTURE

Friday, August 29, 2025

Lamentations 3:37-5

NOTES AND REFLECTIONS

VERSE OF THE DAY LAMENTATIONS 5:21

PRAYER & PRAISE

TODAY I'M GRATEFUL FOR

1.

2.

3.

SEEKING  SCRIPTURE

Saturday, August 30, 2025

NOTES AND REFLECTIONS **Ezekiel 1-4**

Study Notes

VERSE OF THE DAY EZEKIEL 2:7

PRAYER & PRAISE

TODAY I'M GRATEFUL FOR

1.

2.

3.

SEEKING  SCRIPTURE

Sunday, August 31, 2025

Ezekiel 5-8

Study Notes

NOTES AND REFLECTIONS

VERSE OF THE DAY EZEKIEL 6:4

PRAYER & PRAISE

TODAY I'M GRATEFUL FOR

1.

2.

3.

SEEKING SCRIPTURE

Monday, September 1, 2025

NOTES AND REFLECTIONS

Ezekiel 9-12

Study Notes

VERSE OF THE DAY EZEKIEL 11:12

PRAYER & PRAISE

TODAY I'M GRATEFUL FOR

1.

2.

3.

SEEKING SCRIPTURE

Tuesday, September 2, 2025

Ezekiel 13-15

Study Notes

NOTES AND REFLECTIONS

VERSE OF THE DAY EZEKIEL 13:8

TODAY I'M GRATEFUL FOR

1.

2.

3.

PRAYER & PRAISE

SEEKING SCRIPTURE

Wednesday, September 3, 2025

NOTES AND REFLECTIONS   Ezekiel 16-17

Study Notes

VERSE OF THE DAY EZEKIEL 16:59

PRAYER & PRAISE

TODAY I'M GRATEFUL FOR

1.

2.

3.

SEEKING  SCRIPTURE

Thursday, September 4, 2025

Ezekiel 18-20

Study Notes

NOTES AND REFLECTIONS

VERSE OF THE DAY EZEKIEL 18:21

TODAY I'M GRATEFUL FOR

1.

2.

3.

PRAYER & PRAISE

SEEKING  SCRIPTURE

Friday, September 5, 2025

NOTES AND REFLECTIONS **Ezekiel 21-22**

Study Notes

VERSE OF THE DAY EZEKIEL 22:30

PRAYER & PRAISE

TODAY I'M GRATEFUL FOR

1.

2.

3.

SEEKING SCRIPTURE

Saturday, September 6, 2025

Ezekiel 23-24

Study Notes

NOTES AND REFLECTIONS

VERSE OF THE DAY EZEKIEL 24:27

PRAYER & PRAISE

TODAY I'M GRATEFUL FOR

1.

2.

3.

SEEKING  SCRIPTURE

Sunday, September 7, 2025

NOTES AND REFLECTIONS   Ezekiel 25-27

Study Notes

VERSE OF THE DAY EZEKIEL 25:16

PRAYER & PRAISE

TODAY I'M GRATEFUL FOR

1.

2.

3.

SEEKING  SCRIPTURE

Monday, September 8, 2025

Ezekiel 28-30

NOTES AND REFLECTIONS

Study Notes

VERSE OF THE DAY EZEKIEL 28:26

PRAYER & PRAISE

TODAY I'M GRATEFUL FOR

1.

2.

3.

SEEKING SCRIPTURE

Tuesday, September 9, 2025

NOTES AND REFLECTIONS Ezekiel 31-33

Study Notes

VERSE OF THE DAY EZEKIEL 33:7

PRAYER & PRAISE

TODAY I'M GRATEFUL FOR

1.

2.

3.

SEEKING  SCRIPTURE

Wednesday, September 10, 2025

Ezekiel 34-36

NOTES AND REFLECTIONS

Study Notes

VERSE OF THE DAY EZEKIEL 36:26

PRAYER & PRAISE

TODAY I'M GRATEFUL FOR

1.

2.

3.

SEEKING SCRIPTURE

Thursday, September 11, 2025

NOTES AND REFLECTIONS   Ezekiel 37-39

Study Notes

VERSE OF THE DAY EZEKIEL 37:5

PRAYER & PRAISE

TODAY I'M GRATEFUL FOR

1.

2.

3.

SEEKING SCRIPTURE

Friday, September 12, 2025

Ezekiel 40-42

NOTES AND REFLECTIONS

Study Notes

VERSE OF THE DAY EZEKIEL 40:2

TODAY I'M GRATEFUL FOR

1.

2.

3.

PRAYER & PRAISE

SEEKING  SCRIPTURE

Saturday, September 13, 2025

NOTES AND REFLECTIONS   Ezekiel 43-45

Study Notes

VERSE OF THE DAY EZEKIEL 43:5

PRAYER & PRAISE

TODAY I'M GRATEFUL FOR

1.

2.

3.

SEEKING SCRIPTURE

Sunday, September 14, 2025

Ezekiel 46-48

Study Notes

NOTES AND REFLECTIONS

VERSE OF THE DAY EZEKIEL 46:1

TODAY I'M GRATEFUL FOR

1.

2.

3.

PRAYER & PRAISE

SEEKING SCRIPTURE

Monday, September 15, 2025

NOTES AND REFLECTIONS   Daniel 1-3

Study Notes

VERSE OF THE DAY DANIEL 2:47

PRAYER & PRAISE

TODAY I'M GRATEFUL FOR

1.

2.

3.

SEEKING  SCRIPTURE

Tuesday, September 16, 2025

Daniel 4-6

Study Notes

NOTES AND REFLECTIONS

VERSE OF THE DAY DANIEL 4:3

TODAY I'M GRATEFUL FOR

1.

2.

3.

PRAYER & PRAISE

SEEKING SCRIPTURE

Wednesday, September 17, 2025

NOTES AND REFLECTIONS | Daniel 7-9

Study Notes

VERSE OF THE DAY DANIEL 9:5

PRAYER & PRAISE

TODAY I'M GRATEFUL FOR

1.

2.

3.

SEEKING  SCRIPTURE

Thursday, September 18, 2025

Daniel 10-12

Study Notes

NOTES AND REFLECTIONS

VERSE OF THE DAY DANIEL 10:12

TODAY I'M GRATEFUL FOR

1.

2.

3.

PRAYER & PRAISE

SEEKING SCRIPTURE

Friday, September 19, 2025

NOTES AND REFLECTIONS Hosea 1-7

Study Notes

VERSE OF THE DAY HOSEA 6:1

PRAYER & PRAISE

TODAY I'M GRATEFUL FOR

1.

2.

3.

SEEKING SCRIPTURE

Saturday, September 20, 2025

Hosea 8-14

NOTES AND REFLECTIONS

Study Notes

VERSE OF THE DAY HOSEA 14:9

PRAYER & PRAISE

TODAY I'M GRATEFUL FOR

1.

2.

3.

SEEKING  SCRIPTURE

Sunday, September 21, 2025

NOTES AND REFLECTIONS Joel 1-3

Study Notes

VERSE OF THE DAY JOEL 2:13

PRAYER & PRAISE

TODAY I'M GRATEFUL FOR

1.

2.

3.

SEEKING SCRIPTURE

Monday, September 22, 2025

Amos 1-5

Study Notes

NOTES AND REFLECTIONS

VERSE OF THE DAY AMOS 4:13

PRAYER & PRAISE

TODAY I'M GRATEFUL FOR

1.

2.

3.

SEEKING SCRIPTURE

Tuesday, September 23, 2025

NOTES AND REFLECTIONS **Amos 6-9**

Study Notes

VERSE OF THE DAY AMOS 8:11

PRAYER & PRAISE

TODAY I'M GRATEFUL FOR

1.

2.

3.

SEEKING SCRIPTURE

Wednesday, September 24, 2025

Obadiah-Jonah

NOTES AND REFLECTIONS

Study Notes

VERSE OF THE DAY JONAH 2:8-9

PRAYER & PRAISE

TODAY I'M GRATEFUL FOR

1.

2.

3.

SEEKING  SCRIPTURE

Thursday, September 25, 2025

NOTES AND REFLECTIONS　　　　　　　　　　　　Micah 1-7

Study Notes

VERSE OF THE DAY MICAH 4:2

PRAYER & PRAISE

TODAY I'M GRATEFUL FOR

1.

2.

3.

SEEKING SCRIPTURE

Friday, September 26, 2025

Nahum 1-3

Study Notes

NOTES AND REFLECTIONS

VERSE OF THE DAY NAHUM 1:7

PRAYER & PRAISE

TODAY I'M GRATEFUL FOR

1.

2.

3.

SEEKING SCRIPTURE

Saturday, September 27, 2025

NOTES AND REFLECTIONS **Habakkuk-Zephaniah**

Study Notes

VERSE OF THE DAY HABAKKUK 2:4

PRAYER & PRAISE

TODAY I'M GRATEFUL FOR

1.

2.

3.

SEEKING  SCRIPTURE

Sunday, September 28, 2025

Haggai 1-2

Study Notes

NOTES AND REFLECTIONS

VERSE OF THE DAY HAGGAI 2:9

TODAY I'M GRATEFUL FOR

1.

2.

3.

PRAYER & PRAISE

SEEKING  SCRIPTURE

Monday, September 29, 2025

NOTES AND REFLECTIONS   Zechariah 1-7

Study Notes

VERSE OF THE DAY ZECHARIAH 1:16

PRAYER & PRAISE

TODAY I'M GRATEFUL FOR

1.

2.

3.

SEEKING SCRIPTURE

Tuesday, September 30, 2025

Zechariah 8-14

NOTES AND REFLECTIONS

Study Notes

VERSE OF THE DAY ZECHARIAH 8:15

TODAY I'M GRATEFUL FOR

1.

2.

3.

PRAYER & PRAISE

SEEKING SCRIPTURE

Wednesday, October 1, 2025

NOTES AND REFLECTIONS　　　　　　　　**Malachi 1-4**

Study Notes

VERSE OF THE DAY MALACHI 3:6

PRAYER & PRAISE

TODAY I'M GRATEFUL FOR

1.

2.

3.

SEEKING SCRIPTURE

Thursday, October 2, 2025

Matthew 1-4

Study Notes

NOTES AND REFLECTIONS

VERSE OF THE DAY MATTHEW 3:2

TODAY I'M GRATEFUL FOR

1.

2.

3.

PRAYER & PRAISE

SEEKING SCRIPTURE

Friday, October 3, 2025

NOTES AND REFLECTIONS Matthew 5-6

Study Notes

VERSE OF THE DAY MATTHEW 5:17–18

PRAYER & PRAISE

TODAY I'M GRATEFUL FOR

1.

2.

3.

SEEKING  SCRIPTURE

Saturday, October 4, 2025

Matthew 7-8

NOTES AND REFLECTIONS

Study Notes

VERSE OF THE DAY MATTHEW 7:2

PRAYER & PRAISE

TODAY I'M GRATEFUL FOR

1.

2.

3.

SEEKING SCRIPTURE

Sunday, October 5, 2025

NOTES AND REFLECTIONS					Matthew 9-10

Study Notes

VERSE OF THE DAY MATTHEW 9:13

PRAYER & PRAISE

TODAY I'M GRATEFUL FOR

1.

2.

3.

SEEKING  SCRIPTURE

Monday, October 6, 2025

Matthew 11-12

NOTES AND REFLECTIONS

Study Notes

VERSE OF THE DAY MATTHEW 12:36

PRAYER & PRAISE

TODAY I'M GRATEFUL FOR

1.

2.

3.

SEEKING SCRIPTURE

Tuesday, October 7, 2025

NOTES AND REFLECTIONS

Matthew 13-14

Study Notes

VERSE OF THE DAY MATTHEW 14:31

PRAYER & PRAISE

TODAY I'M GRATEFUL FOR

1.

2.

3.

SEEKING  SCRIPTURE

Wednesday, October 8, 2025

Matthew 15-17

Study Notes

NOTES AND REFLECTIONS

VERSE OF THE DAY MATTHEW 15:8–9

PRAYER & PRAISE

TODAY I'M GRATEFUL FOR

1.

2.

3.

SEEKING  SCRIPTURE

Thursday, October 9, 2025

NOTES AND REFLECTIONS Matthew 18-19

Study Notes

VERSE OF THE DAY MATTHEW 19:17

PRAYER & PRAISE

TODAY I'M GRATEFUL FOR

1.

2.

3.

SEEKING  SCRIPTURE

Friday, October 10, 2025

Matthew 20-21

NOTES AND REFLECTIONS

Study Notes

VERSE OF THE DAY MATTHEW 20:28

PRAYER & PRAISE

TODAY I'M GRATEFUL FOR

1.

2.

3.

SEEKING SCRIPTURE

Saturday, October 11, 2025

NOTES AND REFLECTIONS　　　　　　　　Matthew 22-23

Study Notes

VERSE OF THE DAY MATTHEW 23:39

PRAYER & PRAISE

TODAY I'M GRATEFUL FOR

1.

2.

3.

SEEKING  SCRIPTURE

Sunday, October 12, 2025

Matthew 24-25

Study Notes

NOTES AND REFLECTIONS

VERSE OF THE DAY MATTHEW 24:4-5

PRAYER & PRAISE

TODAY I'M GRATEFUL FOR

1.

2.

3.

SEEKING SCRIPTURE

Monday, October 13, 2025

NOTES AND REFLECTIONS Matthew 26

Study Notes

VERSE OF THE DAY MATTHEW 26:10-11

PRAYER & PRAISE

TODAY I'M GRATEFUL FOR

1.

2.

3.

SEEKING  SCRIPTURE

Tuesday, October 14, 2025

Matthew 27-28

Study Notes

NOTES AND REFLECTIONS

VERSE OF THE DAY MATTHEW 27:51-52

TODAY I'M GRATEFUL FOR

1.

2.

3.

PRAYER & PRAISE

SEEKING  SCRIPTURE

Wednesday, October 15, 2025

NOTES AND REFLECTIONS Mark 1-3

Study Notes

VERSE OF THE DAY MARK 2:8

PRAYER & PRAISE

TODAY I'M GRATEFUL FOR

1.

2.

3.

SEEKING SCRIPTURE

Thursday, October 16, 2025

Mark 4-5

Study Notes

NOTES AND REFLECTIONS

VERSE OF THE DAY MARK 4:11

TODAY I'M GRATEFUL FOR

1.

2.

3.

PRAYER & PRAISE

SEEKING  SCRIPTURE

Friday, October 17, 2025

NOTES AND REFLECTIONS **Mark 6-7**

Study Notes

VERSE OF THE DAY MARK 6:50

PRAYER & PRAISE

TODAY I'M GRATEFUL FOR

1.

2.

3.

SEEKING  SCRIPTURE

Saturday, October 18, 2025

Mark 8-9

Study Notes

NOTES AND REFLECTIONS

VERSE OF THE DAY MARK 8:36

TODAY I'M GRATEFUL FOR

1.

2.

3.

PRAYER & PRAISE

SEEKING  SCRIPTURE

Sunday, October 19, 2025

NOTES AND REFLECTIONS Mark 10-11

Study Notes

VERSE OF THE DAY MARK 10:15-16

PRAYER & PRAISE

TODAY I'M GRATEFUL FOR

1.

2.

3.

SEEKING  SCRIPTURE

Monday, October 20, 2025

Mark 12-13

Study Notes

NOTES AND REFLECTIONS

VERSE OF THE DAY MARK 12:24

TODAY I'M GRATEFUL FOR

1.

2.

3.

PRAYER & PRAISE

SEEKING  SCRIPTURE

Tuesday, October 21, 2025

NOTES AND REFLECTIONS   Mark 14

Study Notes

VERSE OF THE DAY MARK 14:62

PRAYER & PRAISE

TODAY I'M GRATEFUL FOR

1.

2.

3.

SEEKING SCRIPTURE

Wednesday, October 22, 2025

Mark 15-16

Study Notes

NOTES AND REFLECTIONS

VERSE OF THE DAY MARK 16:6

TODAY I'M GRATEFUL FOR

1.

2.

3.

PRAYER & PRAISE

SEEKING  SCRIPTURE

Thursday, October 23, 2025

NOTES AND REFLECTIONS   Luke 1

Study Notes

VERSE OF THE DAY LUKE 1:76-77

PRAYER & PRAISE

TODAY I'M GRATEFUL FOR

1.

2.

3.

SEEKING SCRIPTURE

Friday, October 24, 2025

Luke 2-3

Study Notes

NOTES AND REFLECTIONS

VERSE OF THE DAY LUKE 2:11

TODAY I'M GRATEFUL FOR

1.

2.

3.

PRAYER & PRAISE

SEEKING  SCRIPTURE

Saturday, October 25, 2025

NOTES AND REFLECTIONS   Luke 4-5

Study Notes

VERSE OF THE DAY LUKE 4:43

PRAYER & PRAISE

TODAY I'M GRATEFUL FOR

1.

2.

3.

SEEKING SCRIPTURE

Sunday, October 26, 2025

Luke 6-7

Study Notes

NOTES AND REFLECTIONS

VERSE OF THE DAY LUKE 6:35

TODAY I'M GRATEFUL FOR

1.

2.

3.

PRAYER & PRAISE

SEEKING  SCRIPTURE

Monday, October 27, 2025

NOTES AND REFLECTIONS Luke 8-9

Study Notes

VERSE OF THE DAY LUKE 8:21

PRAYER & PRAISE

TODAY I'M GRATEFUL FOR

1.

2.

3.

SEEKING SCRIPTURE

Tuesday, October 28, 2025

Luke 10-11

Study Notes

NOTES AND REFLECTIONS

VERSE OF THE DAY LUKE 11:28

TODAY I'M GRATEFUL FOR

1.

2.

3.

PRAYER & PRAISE

SEEKING SCRIPTURE

Wednesday, October 29, 2025

NOTES AND REFLECTIONS **Luke 12-13**

Study Notes

VERSE OF THE DAY LUKE 12:7

PRAYER & PRAISE

TODAY I'M GRATEFUL FOR

1.

2.

3.

SEEKING SCRIPTURE

Thursday, October 30, 2025

Luke 14-16

Study Notes

NOTES AND REFLECTIONS

VERSE OF THE DAY LUKE 15:7

TODAY I'M GRATEFUL FOR

1.

2.

3.

PRAYER & PRAISE

SEEKING  SCRIPTURE

Friday, October 31, 2025

NOTES AND REFLECTIONS　　　　　　　　　　**Luke 17-18**

Study Notes

VERSE OF THE DAY LUKE 17:15

PRAYER & PRAISE

TODAY I'M GRATEFUL FOR

1.

2.

3.

SEEKING SCRIPTURE

Saturday, November 1, 2025

Luke 19-20

Study Notes

NOTES AND REFLECTIONS

VERSE OF THE DAY LUKE 20:25

PRAYER & PRAISE

TODAY I'M GRATEFUL FOR

1.

2.

3.

SEEKING  SCRIPTURE

Sunday, November 2, 2025

NOTES AND REFLECTIONS **Luke 21-22**

Study Notes

VERSE OF THE DAY LUKE 21:33

PRAYER & PRAISE

TODAY I'M GRATEFUL FOR

1.

2.

3.

SEEKING SCRIPTURE

Monday, November 3, 2025

Luke 23-24

Study Notes

NOTES AND REFLECTIONS

VERSE OF THE DAY LUKE 24:44

TODAY I'M GRATEFUL FOR

1.

2.

3.

PRAYER & PRAISE

SEEKING SCRIPTURE

Tuesday, November 4, 2025

NOTES AND REFLECTIONS

John 1-2

Study Notes

VERSE OF THE DAY JOHN 1:14

PRAYER & PRAISE

TODAY I'M GRATEFUL FOR

1.

2.

3.

SEEKING SCRIPTURE

Wednesday, November 5, 2025

John 3-4

Study Notes

NOTES AND REFLECTIONS

VERSE OF THE DAY JOHN 3:30

PRAYER & PRAISE

TODAY I'M GRATEFUL FOR

1.

2.

3.

SEEKING  SCRIPTURE

Thursday, November 6, 2025

NOTES AND REFLECTIONS　　　　　　　　　　　　John 5-6

Study Notes

VERSE OF THE DAY JOHN 5:46-47

PRAYER & PRAISE

TODAY I'M GRATEFUL FOR

1.

2.

3.

SEEKING SCRIPTURE

Friday, November 7, 2025

John 7-8

Study Notes

NOTES AND REFLECTIONS

VERSE OF THE DAY JOHN 8:28

TODAY I'M GRATEFUL FOR

1.

2.

3.

PRAYER & PRAISE

SEEKING  SCRIPTURE

Saturday, November 8, 2025

NOTES AND REFLECTIONS　　　　　　　　　　　John 9-10

Study Notes

VERSE OF THE DAY JOHN 10:9

PRAYER & PRAISE

TODAY I'M GRATEFUL FOR

1.

2.

3.

SEEKING  SCRIPTURE

Sunday, November 9, 2025

John 11-12

Study Notes

NOTES AND REFLECTIONS

VERSE OF THE DAY JOHN 12:42

PRAYER & PRAISE

TODAY I'M GRATEFUL FOR

1.

2.

3.

SEEKING  SCRIPTURE

Monday, November 10, 2025

NOTES AND REFLECTIONS   John 13-15

Study Notes

VERSE OF THE DAY JOHN 14:21

PRAYER & PRAISE

TODAY I'M GRATEFUL FOR

1.

2.

3.

SEEKING SCRIPTURE

Tuesday, November 11, 2025

John 16-18

Study Notes

NOTES AND REFLECTIONS

VERSE OF THE DAY JOHN 16:33

TODAY I'M GRATEFUL FOR

1.

2.

3.

PRAYER & PRAISE

SEEKING  SCRIPTURE

Wednesday, November 12, 2025

NOTES AND REFLECTIONS

John 19-21

Study Notes

VERSE OF THE DAY JOHN 20:29

PRAYER & PRAISE

TODAY I'M GRATEFUL FOR

1.

2.

3.

SEEKING  SCRIPTURE

Thursday, November 13, 2025

Acts 1-3

NOTES AND REFLECTIONS

Study Notes

VERSE OF THE DAY ACTS 2:42

TODAY I'M GRATEFUL FOR

1.

2.

3.

PRAYER & PRAISE

SEEKING SCRIPTURE

Friday, November 14, 2025

NOTES AND REFLECTIONS Acts 4-6

Study Notes

VERSE OF THE DAY ACTS 5:29

PRAYER & PRAISE

TODAY I'M GRATEFUL FOR

1.

2.

3.

SEEKING SCRIPTURE

Saturday, November 15, 2025

Acts 7-8

Study Notes

NOTES AND REFLECTIONS

VERSE OF THE DAY ACTS 7:56

PRAYER & PRAISE

TODAY I'M GRATEFUL FOR

1.

2.

3.

SEEKING  SCRIPTURE

Sunday, November 16, 2025

NOTES AND REFLECTIONS　　　　　　　　　　　　**Acts 9-10**

Study Notes

VERSE OF THE DAY ACTS 10:34-35

PRAYER & PRAISE

TODAY I'M GRATEFUL FOR

1.

2.

3.

SEEKING  SCRIPTURE

Monday, November 17, 2025

Acts 11-13

NOTES AND REFLECTIONS

Study Notes

VERSE OF THE DAY ACTS 13:52

PRAYER & PRAISE

TODAY I'M GRATEFUL FOR

1.

2.

3.

SEEKING SCRIPTURE

Tuesday, November 18, 2025

NOTES AND REFLECTIONS **Acts 14-15**

Study Notes

VERSE OF THE DAY ACTS 15:32

PRAYER & PRAISE

TODAY I'M GRATEFUL FOR

1.

2.

3.

SEEKING SCRIPTURE

Wednesday, November 19, 2025

Acts 16-17

NOTES AND REFLECTIONS

Study Notes

VERSE OF THE DAY ACTS 17:11

TODAY I'M GRATEFUL FOR

1.

2.

3.

PRAYER & PRAISE

SEEKING SCRIPTURE

Thursday, November 20, 2025

NOTES AND REFLECTIONS **Acts 18-20**

Study Notes

VERSE OF THE DAY ACTS 19:20

PRAYER & PRAISE

TODAY I'M GRATEFUL FOR

1.

2.

3.

SEEKING SCRIPTURE

Friday, November 21, 2025

Acts 21-23

Study Notes

NOTES AND REFLECTIONS

VERSE OF THE DAY ACTS 21:13

PRAYER & PRAISE

TODAY I'M GRATEFUL FOR

1.

2.

3.

SEEKING SCRIPTURE

Saturday, November 22, 2025

NOTES AND REFLECTIONS **Acts 24-26**

Study Notes

VERSE OF THE DAY ACTS 24:14

PRAYER & PRAISE

TODAY I'M GRATEFUL FOR

1.

2.

3.

SEEKING  SCRIPTURE

Sunday, November 23, 2025

Acts 27-28

Study Notes

NOTES AND REFLECTIONS

VERSE OF THE DAY ACTS 28:28

PRAYER & PRAISE

TODAY I'M GRATEFUL FOR

1.

2.

3.

SEEKING  SCRIPTURE

Monday, November 24, 2025

NOTES AND REFLECTIONS   Romans 1-3

Study Notes

VERSE OF THE DAY ROMANS 1:16

PRAYER & PRAISE

TODAY I'M GRATEFUL FOR

1.

2.

3.

SEEKING SCRIPTURE

Tuesday, November 25, 2025

Romans 4-7

Study Notes

NOTES AND REFLECTIONS

VERSE OF THE DAY ROMANS 6:1-2

TODAY I'M GRATEFUL FOR

1.

2.

3.

PRAYER & PRAISE

SEEKING  SCRIPTURE

Wednesday, November 26, 2025

NOTES AND REFLECTIONS　　　　　　　　　　**Romans 8-10**

Study Notes

VERSE OF THE DAY ROMANS 8:7-8

PRAYER & PRAISE

TODAY I'M GRATEFUL FOR

1.

2.

3.

SEEKING SCRIPTURE

Thursday, November 27, 2025

Romans 11-13

Study Notes

NOTES AND REFLECTIONS

VERSE OF THE DAY ROMANS 12:3

TODAY I'M GRATEFUL FOR

1.

2.

3.

PRAYER & PRAISE

SEEKING SCRIPTURE

Friday, November 28, 2025

NOTES AND REFLECTIONS **Romans 14-16**

Study Notes

VERSE OF THE DAY ROMANS 14:4

PRAYER & PRAISE

TODAY I'M GRATEFUL FOR

1.

2.

3.

SEEKING  SCRIPTURE

Saturday, November 29, 2025

1 Corinthians 1-4

Study Notes

NOTES AND REFLECTIONS

VERSE OF THE DAY 1 CORINTHIANS 2:12

PRAYER & PRAISE

TODAY I'M GRATEFUL FOR

1.

2.

3.

SEEKING  SCRIPTURE

Sunday, November 30, 2025

NOTES AND REFLECTIONS   1 Corinthians 5-8

Study Notes

VERSE OF THE DAY 1 CORINTHIANS 8:6

PRAYER & PRAISE

TODAY I'M GRATEFUL FOR

1.

2.

3.

SEEKING  SCRIPTURE

Monday, December 1, 2025

1 Corinthians 9-11

NOTES AND REFLECTIONS

Study Notes

VERSE OF THE DAY 1 CORINTHIANS 10:13

PRAYER & PRAISE

TODAY I'M GRATEFUL FOR

1.

2.

3.

SEEKING  SCRIPTURE

Tuesday, December 2, 2025

NOTES AND REFLECTIONS 1 Corinthians 12-14

Study Notes

VERSE OF THE DAY 1 CORINTHIANS 12:26-27

PRAYER & PRAISE

TODAY I'M GRATEFUL FOR

1.

2.

3.

SEEKING  SCRIPTURE

Wednesday, December 3, 2025

1 Corinthians 15-16

Study Notes

NOTES AND REFLECTIONS

VERSE OF THE DAY 1 CORINTHIANS 15:33-34

TODAY I'M GRATEFUL FOR

1.

2.

3.

PRAYER & PRAISE

SEEKING  SCRIPTURE

Thursday, December 4, 2025

NOTES AND REFLECTIONS **2 Corinthians 1-4**

Study Notes

VERSE OF THE DAY 2 CORINTHIANS 4:6

PRAYER & PRAISE

TODAY I'M GRATEFUL FOR

1.

2.

3.

SEEKING SCRIPTURE

Friday, December 5, 2025

2 Corinthians 5-9

Study Notes

NOTES AND REFLECTIONS

VERSE OF THE DAY 2 CORINTHIANS 6:17-18

PRAYER & PRAISE

TODAY I'M GRATEFUL FOR

1.

2.

3.

SEEKING  SCRIPTURE

Saturday, December 6, 2025

NOTES AND REFLECTIONS **2 Corinthians 10-13**

Study Notes

VERSE OF THE DAY 2 CORINTHIANS 13:5

PRAYER & PRAISE

TODAY I'M GRATEFUL FOR

1.

2.

3.

SEEKING SCRIPTURE

Sunday, December 7, 2025

Galatians 1-3

Study Notes

NOTES AND REFLECTIONS

VERSE OF THE DAY GALATIANS 2:20

PRAYER & PRAISE

TODAY I'M GRATEFUL FOR

1.

2.

3.

SEEKING SCRIPTURE

Monday, December 8, 2025

NOTES AND REFLECTIONS   Galatians 4-6

Study Notes

VERSE OF THE DAY GALATIANS 5:7

PRAYER & PRAISE

TODAY I'M GRATEFUL FOR

1.

2.

3.

SEEKING SCRIPTURE

Tuesday, December 9, 2025

Ephesians 1-3

NOTES AND REFLECTIONS

Study Notes

VERSE OF THE DAY EPHESIANS 2:8

TODAY I'M GRATEFUL FOR

1.

2.

3.

PRAYER & PRAISE

SEEKING  SCRIPTURE

Wednesday, December 10, 2025

NOTES AND REFLECTIONS   Ephesians 4-6

Study Notes

VERSE OF THE DAY EPHESIANS 4:32

PRAYER & PRAISE

TODAY I'M GRATEFUL FOR

1.

2.

3.

SEEKING  SCRIPTURE

Thursday, December 11, 2025

Philippians 1-4

Study Notes

NOTES AND REFLECTIONS

VERSE OF THE DAY PHILIPPIANS 2:12

TODAY I'M GRATEFUL FOR

1.

2.

3.

PRAYER & PRAISE

SEEKING  SCRIPTURE

Friday, December 12, 2025

NOTES AND REFLECTIONS　　　　　　　　　　**Colossians 1-4**

Study Notes

VERSE OF THE DAY COLOSSIANS 3:17

PRAYER & PRAISE

TODAY I'M GRATEFUL FOR

1.

2.

3.

SEEKING  SCRIPTURE

Saturday, December 13, 2025

1 Thessalonians 1-5

NOTES AND REFLECTIONS

Study Notes

VERSE OF THE DAY 1 THESSALONIANS 3:12

PRAYER & PRAISE

TODAY I'M GRATEFUL FOR

1.

2.

3.

SEEKING  SCRIPTURE

Sunday, December 14, 2025

NOTES AND REFLECTIONS

2 Thessalonians 1-3

Study Notes

VERSE OF THE DAY 2 THESSALONIANS 1:11

PRAYER & PRAISE

TODAY I'M GRATEFUL FOR

1.

2.

3.

SEEKING  SCRIPTURE

Monday, December 15, 2025

1 Timothy 1-6

NOTES AND REFLECTIONS

Study Notes

VERSE OF THE DAY 1 TIMOTHY 4:7-8

PRAYER & PRAISE

TODAY I'M GRATEFUL FOR

1.

2.

3.

SEEKING  SCRIPTURE

Tuesday, December 16, 2025

NOTES AND REFLECTIONS **2 Timothy 1-4**

Study Notes

VERSE OF THE DAY 2 TIMOTHY 1:14

PRAYER & PRAISE

TODAY I'M GRATEFUL FOR

1.

2.

3.

SEEKING  SCRIPTURE

Wednesday, December 17, 2025

Titus-Philemon

Study Notes

NOTES AND REFLECTIONS

VERSE OF THE DAY TITUS 2:7–8

PRAYER & PRAISE

TODAY I'M GRATEFUL FOR

1.

2.

3.

SEEKING SCRIPTURE

Thursday, December 18, 2025

NOTES AND REFLECTIONS

Hebrews 1-6

Study Notes

VERSE OF THE DAY HEBREWS 2:1

PRAYER & PRAISE

TODAY I'M GRATEFUL FOR

1.

2.

3.

SEEKING  SCRIPTURE

Friday, December 19, 2025

Hebrews 7-10

Study Notes

NOTES AND REFLECTIONS

VERSE OF THE DAY HEBREWS 7:26

PRAYER & PRAISE

TODAY I'M GRATEFUL FOR

1.

2.

3.

SEEKING SCRIPTURE

Saturday, December 20, 2025

NOTES AND REFLECTIONS   **Hebrews 11-13**

Study Notes

VERSE OF THE DAY HEBREWS 12:1-2

PRAYER & PRAISE

TODAY I'M GRATEFUL FOR

1.

2.

3.

SEEKING SCRIPTURE

Sunday, December 21, 2025

James 1-5

NOTES AND REFLECTIONS

Study Notes

VERSE OF THE DAY JAMES 2:18

PRAYER & PRAISE

TODAY I'M GRATEFUL FOR

1.

2.

3.

SEEKING  SCRIPTURE

Monday, December 22, 2025

NOTES AND REFLECTIONS **1 Peter 1-5**

Study Notes

VERSE OF THE DAY 1 PETER 1:14-16

PRAYER & PRAISE

TODAY I'M GRATEFUL FOR

1.

2.

3.

SEEKING  SCRIPTURE

Tuesday, December 23, 2025

2 Peter 1-3

NOTES AND REFLECTIONS

Study Notes

VERSE OF THE DAY 2 PETER 3:9

PRAYER & PRAISE

TODAY I'M GRATEFUL FOR

1.

2.

3.

SEEKING SCRIPTURE

Wednesday, December 24, 2025

NOTES AND REFLECTIONS 1 John 1-5

Study Notes

VERSE OF THE DAY 1 JOHN 2:3-4

PRAYER & PRAISE

TODAY I'M GRATEFUL FOR

1.

2.

3.

SEEKING SCRIPTURE

Thursday, December 25, 2025

2 John-Jude

Study Notes

NOTES AND REFLECTIONS

VERSE OF THE DAY 2 JOHN 1:6

PRAYER & PRAISE

TODAY I'M GRATEFUL FOR

1.

2.

3.

SEEKING SCRIPTURE

Friday, December 26, 2025

NOTES AND REFLECTIONS   Revelation 1-3

Study Notes

VERSE OF THE DAY REVELATION 1:8

PRAYER & PRAISE

TODAY I'M GRATEFUL FOR

1.

2.

3.

SEEKING SCRIPTURE

Saturday, December 27, 2025

Revelation 4-8

Study Notes

NOTES AND REFLECTIONS

VERSE OF THE DAY REVELATION 4:2

TODAY I'M GRATEFUL FOR

1.

2.

3.

PRAYER & PRAISE

SEEKING SCRIPTURE

Sunday, December 28, 2025

NOTES AND REFLECTIONS   **Revelation 9-12**

Study Notes

VERSE OF THE DAY REVELATION 11:3

PRAYER & PRAISE

TODAY I'M GRATEFUL FOR

1.

2.

3.

SEEKING SCRIPTURE

Monday, December 29, 2025

Revelation 13-16

Study Notes

NOTES AND REFLECTIONS

VERSE OF THE DAY REVELATION 14:1

TODAY I'M GRATEFUL FOR

1.

2.

3.

PRAYER & PRAISE

SEEKING SCRIPTURE

Tuesday, December 30, 2025

NOTES AND REFLECTIONS **Revelation 17-19**

Study Notes

VERSE OF THE DAY REVELATION 19:6

PRAYER & PRAISE

TODAY I'M GRATEFUL FOR

1.

2.

3.

SEEKING SCRIPTURE

Wednesday, December 31, 2025

Revelation 20-22

Study Notes

NOTES AND REFLECTIONS

VERSE OF THE DAY REVELATION 22:3

PRAYER & PRAISE

TODAY I'M GRATEFUL FOR

1.

2.

3.

To MaryAnne,
You brought forth strength from weakness,
joy from sadness, and hope from despair.
I look forward to hearing your laughter again.
You are so missed.

Visit us online
SeekingScripture.com

Read our Charter &
Statement of Purpose

Request to join our Discussion Group*

*We only admit new members to our Facebook discussion group during the month of December, just before the new reading cycle starts. We reccommend requesting to join as soon as possible.

SEEKING SCRIPTURE
Bible Reading Checklist
Track your progress

- [ ] Genesis
- [ ] Exodus
- [ ] Leviticus
- [ ] Numbers
- [ ] Deuteronomy
- [ ] Joshua
- [ ] Judges
- [ ] Ruth
- [ ] 1 Samuel
- [ ] 2 Samuel
- [ ] 1 Kings
- [ ] 2 Kings
- [ ] 1 Chronicles
- [ ] 2 Chronicles
- [ ] Ezra
- [ ] Nehemiah
- [ ] Esther
- [ ] Job
- [ ] Psalms
- [ ] Proverbs
- [ ] Ecclesiastes
- [ ] Song of Solomon
- [ ] Isaiah
- [ ] Jeremiah
- [ ] Lamentations
- [ ] Ezekiel
- [ ] Daniel
- [ ] Hosea
- [ ] Joel
- [ ] Amos
- [ ] Obadiah
- [ ] Jonah
- [ ] Micah
- [ ] Nahum
- [ ] Habakkuk
- [ ] Zephaniah
- [ ] Haggai
- [ ] Zechariah
- [ ] Malachi
- [ ] Matthew
- [ ] Mark
- [ ] Luke
- [ ] John
- [ ] Acts
- [ ] Romans
- [ ] 1 Corinthians
- [ ] 2 Corinthians
- [ ] Galatians
- [ ] Ephesians
- [ ] Philippians
- [ ] Colossians
- [ ] 1 Thessalonians
- [ ] 2 Thessalonians
- [ ] 1 Timothy
- [ ] 2 Timothy
- [ ] Titus
- [ ] Philemon
- [ ] Hebrews
- [ ] James
- [ ] 1 Peter
- [ ] 2 Peter
- [ ] 1 John
- [ ] 2 John
- [ ] 3 John
- [ ] Jude
- [ ] Revelation

Made in United States
Orlando, FL
04 December 2024